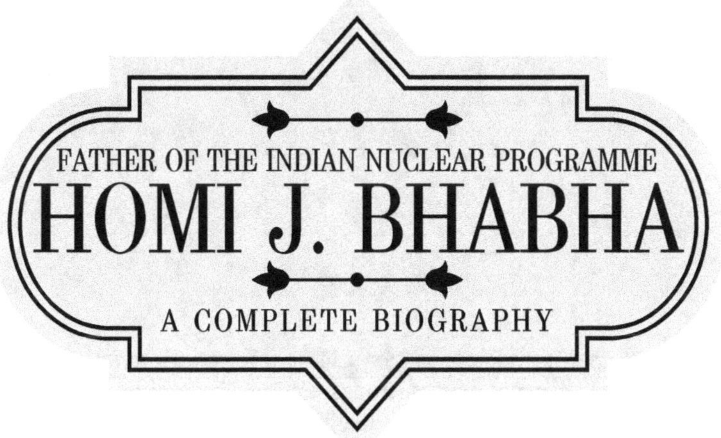

PRASHANT KUMAR

Published by
PRABHAT PRAKASHAN PVT. LTD.
4/19 Asaf Ali Road,
New Delhi-110 002 (INDIA)
e-mail: prabhatbooks@gmail.com

ISBN 978-93-5562-943-2

HOMI J. BHABHA: A COMPLETE BIOGRAPHY
by Prashant Kumar

© Reserved

Edition
First, 2024

Price
₹ 350 (Rupees Three Hundred Fifty Only)

Printed at
Sanjay Printers, Sahibabad

Author's Note

Homi Jehangir Bhabha was a prodigiously talented Indian nuclear physicist whose impact echoes through modern India's advances in science and technology. Often referred to as the father of India's nuclear program, he offers an exemplary narrative of a nation rebuilding and reforming in the aftermath of colonial rule.

Through this book, I aimed to illuminate the development of scientific reasoning in a newly independent India. Bhabha negotiated critical technological partnerships and set in motion seminal nuclear research that aided India's self-reliance and energy security. However, as a vociferous supporter of nuclear disarmament who recognized the threats posed by weapons of mass destruction, Bhabha's worldview extended far beyond nationalistic goals. His life demonstrates an uncompromising adherence to science being utilized to forward human progress and peace.

Dr. Bhabha, endowed with versatile talents, played a crucial role in steering modern science in India towards new horizons. It is due to his foresight that research is now progressing not only in physics but also in various other fields of science, such as electronics, space science, radio astronomy, and molecular biology.

However, Dr. Bhabha's interests and brilliance were not confined to any limits. He was a great visionary, institution builder, administrator, art and beauty enthusiast, and a lover of nature. The unprecedented progress in the scientific and technological development of the country during his tenure of just twenty-five years can be attributed to his work style, diligence, and impactful personality.

This book is for those who have a keen desire to acquire knowledge. It not only presents the biography of Dr. Bhabha but also provides detailed information about his research works in a lucid and enlightening language. It is hoped that this book will succeed in igniting a passion for science among people of all age groups, especially becoming a guiding and inspiring source for the new generation in India.

Contents

Bhabha and His Roots

The Parsi community in India has a rich and fascinating history that can be traced back to ancient Persia (modern-day Iran). The story of the Parsis begins with Zoroastrianism, one of the world's oldest monotheistic religions, founded by the prophet Zarathustra (Zoroaster) in ancient Persia around the 6th century BCE.

Zoroastrianism teaches the existence of one supreme God, Ahura Mazda, and emphasises principles of good thoughts, good words, and good deeds. The ancient Persians practiced Zoroastrianism and revered it as their primary religion.

However, the history of the Parsi community takes a significant turn during the Arab conquest of Persia in the 7th century CE. With the conquest, Islam became the dominant religion, and Zoroastrians faced religious persecution and pressure to convert to Islam. This forced many Zoroastrians to leave their homeland in search of religious freedom and safety.

The Parsis, a group of Zoroastrian migrants, left Persia to escape the religious intolerance and suppression they faced under Muslim rule. They set sail and migrated to various regions, with a significant number of them settling in the Indian subcontinent, particularly in the coastal region of Gujarat.

Historically, the first group of Zoroastrian refugees, believed to be led by a priest named Sanjan, arrived on the shores of Gujarat in the 8th century CE. The local Hindu king, Jadi Rana, welcomed them and granted them asylum, allowing them to practice their religion freely and follow their customs and traditions.

To express their gratitude and commitment to the land that provided them refuge, the Parsis adopted the Gujarati language and assimilated into the local culture while maintaining their distinct Zoroastrian identity.

But these are just a few narratives among many accounts surrounding the Parsis in India. However, our focus on the Parsis stems from our exploration of Homi Bhabha, a distinguished scientist who hailed from the Parsi community. To truly comprehend Homi Bhabha, we must first delve into an understanding of the Parsi community in India.

In the early 17th century, Surat served as a significant base for the Parsi community, and the British chose this city to establish their first factory. The Parsis quickly acquired proficiency in English and became valuable translators for the British, fostering close ties with them. Initially, they engaged with the British as interpreters, hawkers, traders, and contractors. As the 18th century unfolded, they evolved into commercial agents, handling a broad spectrum of activities, including extending credits and procuring ships.

A pivotal figure in this transformative journey was Lovji Nusserwanjee Wadia, who initiated the migration of influential shipbuilders from Surat to Bombay around 1730. Consequently,

Bombay emerged as the new commercial hub for the Parsis. The Parsis transitioned from being mere artisans to ship owners, embarking on trading ventures initially along the Malabar coast and eventually engaging in highly profitable trade with China. The absence of caste prejudices, freedom to navigate the seas, linguistic aptitude, and a reputation for integrity all contributed to their success in lucrative overseas trade with China, leading to the accumulation of considerable wealth.

During this period, numerous Parsi families amassed fortunes, with many recognising the potential benefits of engaging in trade with China, given its status as the most valuable branch of commerce in Bombay. As the Parsis embraced the opium trade, they furthered their economic standing.

The incorporation of Parsis into the economic and political sphere of British power from the late 18th century marked a successful transformation, shifting from a minority community in a provincial setting to an influential colonial elite in Bombay. The Parsis' collaboration with the British was underpinned by a keen understanding of the opportunities presented, benefiting both individuals in direct contact with the British and the Parsi community at large. Their astute navigation of these opportunities facilitated their ascent in the economic and political landscape of colonial India.

The Parsis played a pioneering role in advancing education in Bombay due to their wealth and suitability for such endeavours. Their affluence gave rise to a generation of Parsis well-prepared to lead the community's advancement. Education became a fundamental aspect of Parsi identity, resulting in both social advantage and cultural identification. The subsequent generation, being well-educated, came to recognise themselves as Indians first and Parsis later, instilling a sense of nationalism. Despite being considered among the most loyal colonial subjects, individuals from the Parsi community, within their ranks, laid the foundation for India's self-government.

But not every Parsi family had such thoughts about India. The prosperity of Parsis in Bombay led to an increasing alignment with Western values, identifying closely with the British and fostering a heightened awareness of a broader cosmopolitan identity within the Parsi community. As the economy of Bombay flourished, their loyalties leaned towards the colonisers. This loyalty often led many affluent Parsis in Bombay to adopt an anglophile stance, somewhat detached from Indian culture, society, and their roots in Gujarat.

A significant hallmark of Parsi religion and community is its emphasis on charity, a defining feature deeply ingrained in the community's conscience. This emphasis on charity profoundly influenced the development of Parsi communities in Gujarat and Bombay, particularly during the 19th and 20th centuries. It provided the financial means to establish essential infrastructure, not only in terms of fire temples but also hospitals, libraries, schools, technical colleges, housing colonies, and rest homes for the elderly. The records show significant contributions from notable Parsi families like the Tatas and the Boudris, who donated substantial sums of money to various funds, including the Gandhi Memorial Fund and the Indian Defence Fund during the Indo-Chinese war of 1962.

Homi Jehangir Bhabha, a prominent figure in the scientific world, was born into a family that held a privileged position in Parsi society. His birth took place on Saturday, 30 October 1909, in Bombay. The family residence was a bungalow named "Kenilworth" situated at 53 Pedder Road in South Bombay, which belonged to Bhabha's maternal aunts. In adherence to Parsi customs at the time, the first sound of a newborn's name was astrologically determined, and this led to the selection of the name "Homi," which signified "child lock" for Bhabha. Another theory surrounding his name is the influence of his grandfather's name, Hormusji, which was shortened to "Homi."

Adding to the family, five years later on 21 August 1914, another son named Jamshed was born, who later made significant contributions to art and culture in Bombay. The Bhabha family, while financially comfortable, was not extraordinarily wealthy. Nonetheless, they upheld a strong tradition of learning and service, particularly in the realm of education. Homi Bhabha's paternal grandfather had a notable association with Mysore, dating back to 1876 when he was appointed as the vice principal of Central College in Bangalore. Over the years, he held significant roles in education, culminating in his appointment as the first Indian Inspector General of Education in the state of Mysore from 1895 to 1909. This family heritage of education and service likely played a role in shaping Homi Bhabha's trajectory and commitment to intellectual pursuits.

There's no denying that being born into a privileged family provided Homi a significant advantage in life. Yet, there was an undeniable fire within him, and his potential was apparent. Homi Bhabha was shaped by two influential forces: external conditions and his innate intellectual vigour. Growing up, the intellectual atmosphere at home was as stimulating as any gifted child could hope for. He was encouraged from a young age to appreciate the fine arts, fostering a passion that encompassed all aspects of his life.

His love for art included a deep thirst for Western music and culture, which intensified as he grew older. In his early 20s, he would spend a considerable amount of time at concerts in England, immersing himself in the compositions of his favourite artists. Homi's early affinity for music was notable, as his parents could calm him down by simply playing music, reflecting an innate ear for melodies. The family possessed an extensive collection of Western classical music records, exposing Homi from a young age to the works of eminent European musicians. This passion for Western classical music was further nurtured by his handicapped maternal aunt, who had an impressive collection of 78 RPM gramophone records. Together with his younger brother and cousin, Homi would spend hours listening to these records.

The young Homi not only immersed himself in music but also displayed a fondness for playing the violin and piano. He also enjoyed playing with Meccano, a construction toy, showcasing exceptional skills in designing structures beyond what was included in the accompanying booklet. His father recognised this aptitude and envisioned him becoming an engineer. Though details about Homi Bhabha's childhood are limited, it's evident that he had a diverse range of skills and interests.

Unlike his friend Oppenheimer, whose intellectual prowess far surpassed his years but struggled with social interactions, Bhabha did not create the same sense of separation between himself and others. Although he lived a luxurious and sheltered life, he remained friendly and approachable. While his upbringing wasn't marked by overt emphasis on intelligence, it was undeniably a life of privilege, shaping the trajectory of the remarkable scientist he would become.

Homi Bhabha's artistic talents flourished, and he became a highly skilled artist during his formative years. As a young boy, he consistently won prizes for his drawings at annual exhibitions organised by the Bombay Art Society. Under the guidance of artist Jahangir Lalkaka, he honed his painting skills. Remarkably, at the age of 17, his self-portrait garnered a prize at an exhibition by the Bombay Art Society. His sketches were of such quality that Air India later designed a calendar based on them. Renowned artist MF Hussain even likened Bhabha's lines to those of the great Leonardo da Vinci. Bhabha's knowledge of classical European painters was extensive, showcasing a level of understanding that could have made him an art critic in his own right.

In the arts, Bhabha's understanding and proficiency were so impressive that he was deemed by some as the modern equivalent of Leonardo da Vinci, a comparison made by Rahman during an address to an audience of Indian scientists in Nagpur in 1941. However, notably absent from his artistic repertoire at this stage was any mention or appreciation of Indian art. Growing up in Bombay during the early 20th century, Bhabha seemingly had access to Indian art, but its omission from his interests suggests a high level of Anglophilia. During his youth, art, music, and poetry primarily meant those of Western origin. He drew inspiration from the great Western classics, with figures like Shakespeare serving as his role models.

Bhabha's father, Jahangir, an Oxford-educated individual, commenced his career in Mysore by joining the judicial service of the state. Later, he became a legal adviser to the House of Tatas and served on the board of directors of many Tata companies. He shared a deep appreciation for Western classical music and painting, along with a keen interest in flowers, trees, and gardens. These interests were inherited by young Bhabha, who enjoyed a privileged childhood, receiving not only formal education in school but a substantial portion of his intellectual and artistic education at home. This esteemed pedigree denoted elegance, wealth, and membership in India's academic and artistic elite, playing a crucial role in shaping Bhabha's life and pursuits.

Jehangir Bhabha entered into marriage with Meherbai Panday. Bhabhas also had ties with Tata family. Bhabha's paternal aunt, Meherbai Bhabha (often referred to as "Mehri"), was married to Sir Dorabji Tata, the elder son of Jamsetji Tata. Interestingly, it's believed that Jamsetji played a role in the selection of Meherbai as his daughter-in-law. He frequently visited Mysore from 1880 onwards, recognising the industrial potential of the state. During these visits, he met and befriended Hormusji Bhabha, adding a layer of Tata family connections to the Bhabha family.

After their marriage, Jehangir and Meherbai moved to Bombay from Mysore. Their home housed an extensive collection of books, a compilation of both parents' collections.

Bhabha's parents, Hormusji and Jehangir, had amassed a wide array of books covering literature, education, arts, scientific and technical subjects. Jahangir, during his student days, collected books on painting, further enriching the collection. As his interests expanded to flowers, trees, gardens, and later, science and mathematics due to his prodigious intelligence, the book collection evolved accordingly.

Their home also featured a garden and was adorned with the presence of dogs. It became apparent from an early age that Bhabha possessed exceptional intelligence, prompting his parents to actively nurture and stimulate his burgeoning intellectual and artistic pursuits. Even as a child, Homi Bhabha required little sleep, and despite the family doctor's recommendations, his curiosity and thirst for knowledge continued to flourish. This supportive environment played a vital role in shaping Bhabha's intellect and passion for the sciences and the arts.

The Bhabha family provided an exceptionally nurturing environment for young Homi, not only in terms of education and culture but also in the closeness of their bond as a married couple. He cherished the fact that his parents had a profoundly happy marriage, as the overall happiness and stability of the household were crucial during his formative years. Homi believed that growing up in an atmosphere devoid of anxiety, strain, and hostility was of paramount importance. He considered himself fortunate to be raised in such a wonderful environment, enhanced by the presence of beloved family dogs.

The two brothers, Homi and Jamshed, also shared a very tight-knit bond. According to journalist and author Shyam Bhatia, there were varying perspectives on their relationship. While some saw Jamshed as somewhat jealous of Homi's success and recognition, others emphasised the deep affection and mentorship Homi provided to Jamshed. Nevertheless, it remains a subject of speculation, as Tata's colleagues noted that Jamshed rarely spoke of his elder brother.

Homi deeply cherished the bonds of affection he shared with his parents. After the passing of his father in 1942, he expressed in a letter to a close friend that he felt a void in his heart. Every summer, he made it a point to take his mother on vacation, valuing and cherishing the time spent with her. Even in her later years, Meherbai maintained her grace and elegance, dressing impeccably and showcasing refined fashion choices.

Homi Sethna, who was Chairman of the Atomic Energy Commission from 1972 to 1983 and knew the Bhabha family personally, spoke highly of Meherbai. He described her as an extremely gracious lady who epitomised nobility. Homi Bhabha made it a ritual to see her before leaving for the office every day, endearingly nicknaming her "Twit." Their family dynamic and deep-rooted affections played an influential role in shaping Homi Bhabha's personal and professional life.

Bhabha received his early education at the Cathedral and John Cannon Boys School in Bombay. Interestingly, the grand Esplanade House, the residence of Jamsetji Tata, was nearby to Bhabha's school. He would have his lunch there and spend many fruitful hours in the well-stocked library. In addition to this, the rich library of Dorabji Tata, available for his reference, further enriched his reading experiences. The affection they received from their aunt, Meherbai Tata, who was childless, was akin to that reserved for sons.

Being an avid and voracious reader, Bhabha was particularly captivated by science, although his reading was wide-ranging, laying the foundation for his multifaceted interests and subsequent achievements. An early photograph of Bhabha as an adolescent portrays him dressed in a black suit and tie, a formal pose, with a book on El Greco in his lap, showcasing his love for reading.

Meherbai Tata, their aunt, was a woman of remarkable talents, serving as a perfect complement to Dorabji. She was a champion tennis player, making waves by competing and winning tournaments dressed in a sari, a sight that intrigued many spectators. She even represented India at the Paris Olympics in 1924 and was a familiar face at Wimbledon. Beyond sports, she displayed proficiency in various domains—riding horses, driving motor cars, and playing the piano skillfully, making her sought after for public concerts. Additionally, she owned the renowned Jubilee diamond, a gift from her husband, which is the 6th largest diamond globally, weighing 245.35 carats.

Meherbai Tata was deeply committed to various causes, actively participating in raising contributions during the First World War and serving as an active member of the Indian Red Cross Society. Her concerns for women's conditions led her to advocate for the enactment of the Sarda Act, also known as the Child Marriage Restraint Act, after 1929. This Act aimed to combat child marriages. She campaigned extensively for this Act both in India and abroad. Beyond the Sarda Act, she played a crucial role in advocating for woman suffrage, girls' education, and the elimination of the "corridor system" in education. Unfortunately, Meherbai passed away from leukaemia in 1931 in Wales, and she was laid to rest at the Brookwood Cemetery in Surrey, leaving behind a legacy of significant contributions to the advancement of women in India.

Bhabha was undoubtedly fortunate to be born into a family that not only recognised his talents but also had the means and willingness to nurture them. Additionally, his close association with the Tatas proved to be a significant stroke of luck, as it allowed him to witness the burgeoning world of Indian industry and interact with influential nationalist politicians of the time. Gandhi, Vallabhbhai Patel, Motilal Nehru, and Jawaharlal Nehru were frequent visitors to the Tata home, and Gandhi even stayed with them during the launch of the first civil disobedience movement.

By the time Bhabha went abroad at the age of 18, he already possessed a deep understanding of the ways in which his community could thrive in the evolving political landscape.

He had met foreign leaders and observed the adaptability and strategic approaches of Indian nationalists. Remarkably, even at a young age, he had delved into Einstein's Special Theory of Relativity, a complex subject understood by very few at that time. Bhabha's ability to think in abstract terms and comprehend the limitations of perceiving the natural world solely through ordinary senses was extraordinary.

Bhabha's academic achievements were exceptional. He passed his Cambridge Local Examination Junior in 1924 with honours, securing the Headmaster's Prize for English essay and the Hudson Prize for mathematics. Even his old headmaster, C.H. Hammond, recognised Bhabha's eminence and wrote to congratulate him on his accomplishments, expressing pride in having played a role, no matter how small, in his education.

Upon finishing school at the young age of 15, Bhabha faced a wait to go to Cambridge due to the university's minimum age requirement of 18. In the interim, he spent the academic year 1925-1926 at Elphinstone College, studying arts, and continued his education at the Royal Institute of Science for the BSc class in 1926-1927. In 1927, as Bhabha prepared for Cambridge, a pivotal event occurred in the scientific community: Compton won the Nobel Prize in Physics for his ground-breaking discovery of the Compton effect, providing conclusive evidence of light's particle properties, a sensational revelation during that period.

Thus, began Bhabha's fascinating journey, commencing with mechanical engineering and progressing to mathematics, theoretical physics, and beyond, ultimately shaping the course of scientific history.

Early Education and
Journey to His Peak

Homi Jehangir Bhabha, the renowned figure in the world of science, was born into a family of privilege and education. He entered the world on a Saturday, at Kenilworth on 53 Pedder Road in South Bombay, belonging to his maternal aunts, Bachubai, Hirabai, and later, Cooverbai Panday. In a customary Hindu practice, the first sound of a newborn's name was astrologically determined, aiming to bring luck. While it's uncertain if his parents, Jehangir and Meherbai Bhabha, were believers in this custom, they named him Hormusji after his grandfather. However, he was widely known as Homi among acquaintances, the name under which he gained national and international recognition.

Five years later, another son, Jamshed, was born, making his mark in the realm of art and culture in Bombay. The Bhabha family, although not immensely wealthy, boasted a rich heritage of learning and commitment to education. Homi's paternal grandfather, Hormusji Bhabha, played a pivotal role in the field of education, establishing a legacy that Homi would later follow. Hormusji's association with Mysore commenced in 1876 when he became the vice principal of Central College in Bangalore. This connection endured when, over sixty years later, Homi became a guest lecturer in physics at the same college.

Hormusji's tenure as headmaster of Maharaja's College in Mysore and his subsequent roles in educational reform solidified his influence. His commitment earned him the title of Munir-ul-Taleem from the Mysore government in 1909. Beyond his professional contributions, Hormusji was an influential figure in his community, actively engaged in various associations and committees, fostering progress in the princely state of Mysore.

Hormusji's forward-thinking nature was evident in his support for Bella in the notable 'Saklat vs Bella' case, a significant legal battle regarding the acceptance of a child born to a Parsi mother and non-Parsi father into the Zoroastrian faith. Although this case concluded against Bella, it left a contentious question unresolved about the acceptance of children in similar circumstances into the Zoroastrian community.

Homi, as a Bhabha, undoubtedly enjoyed the advantages of his lineage. However, his inner drive and intellectual prowess played a significant role in shaping him. His upbringing was intellectually enriching, fostering an aristocratic appreciation for the arts from an early age. His passion for Western music and culture continued to flourish, and in his early twenties, he spent considerable time attending concerts in England, immersing himself in the works of his favourite composers.

The confluence of external influences and his inherent energy marked Homi Bhabha's formative years, igniting a fire within him that burned brightly, propelling him towards an exceptional destiny in the realms of science and culture.

Homi Jehangir Bhabha's fondness for music was apparent from an early age. It was said that the mere sound of music was enough to soothe him as an infant. His family's extensive collection of Western classical music records allowed him to become immersed in the works of prominent European composers from a young age. Living with his maternal aunt, Cooverbai, who had a remarkable assortment of 78 RPM gramophone records, added a delightful dimension to his musical education. Hindered by physical disabilities and unable to move independently, Cooverbai shared her cherished collection with Homi, his younger brother, and their cousin, Dinshaw Panday, fostering their deep appreciation for music.

Listening to compositions by the likes of Beethoven, Mozart, Bach, Haydn, Verdi, Wagner, and Schubert, the young trio took turns to operate the gramophone, absorbing the nuances of symphonies and concertos. By the age of eight, Homi was well-versed not only in the works of Beethoven but also Mozart, Verdi, and Wagner, laying the foundation for his enduring love for symphonic and operatic music. His enthusiasm for music extended to attending concerts in various cities like Vienna, Boston, and Bombay, solidifying his passion and understanding of Western classical music. Meanwhile, his brother, Jamshed, became a lifelong devotee of Beethoven, commemorated by an Indian postage stamp in his honour.

Beyond music, Homi's inquisitive mind and creativity were evident in his childhood pursuits. His father, who aspired for him to become an engineer, provided him with Meccano sets, which Homi used not only to construct models from the provided booklet but also to explore models of his own design. However, this curiosity almost led to a grave mishap when, inspired by the concept of parachutes during World War I, he and his cousin attempted a daring 'parachute' experiment from a balcony. Fortunately, an older cousin intervened in time, averting disaster. These anecdotes hint at an almost precocious inclination towards daring experimentation.

Although his upbringing was affluent and sheltered, it's unclear whether Homi experienced typical childhood escapades and mischief. While he didn't exhibit the same social detachment as his contemporary, J. Robert Oppenheimer, it's noted that Homi maintained a friendly yet reserved demeanour, keeping a measured distance from most people.

Apart from his musical talents and scientific acumen, Homi displayed remarkable artistic abilities, earning prizes for his drawings at the Bombay Art Society's annual exhibitions. His self-portrait won accolades when he was just 17. His sketches were so impressive that they were used for an Air India calendar, and the renowned artist MF Husain admired his artistry, comparing his lines to Leonardo da Vinci's. His extensive knowledge of classical European painters and artistry positioned him as an astute critic in the art world. However, at this stage, there is a noticeable absence of mention of Indian art in his repertoire, indicative of a strong inclination towards Western art.

Despite his seemingly dominant fascination with Western culture in his youth, Homi was well-versed in Indian history. His letters to his friend Homi Seervai reflected his keen interest in how history should be documented in India, hinting at a broader understanding of his cultural roots amid his overwhelming exposure to Western art, music, and literature.

Homi Jehangir Bhabha's exposure to Western art and culture primarily stemmed from his father's extensive collection of books on the subject. However, it was his personal experiences in European museums and galleries during family vacations that significantly shaped his appreciation for great works of art. While these exposures influenced his early artistic inclinations, it was during his return from England that his admiration for Indian art began to flourish.

Although his childhood was steeped in a rich amalgamation of Western artistic and cultural influences, it was his stay in Bangalore that allowed him to explore and appreciate Indian art and music. Attending Hindustani and Carnatic music concerts, Bhabha developed a deep admiration for acclaimed figures in Carnatic music, including A.R. Iyengar and M.S. Subbulakshmi. This growing attachment to Indian cultural traditions and heritage played a crucial role in shaping his later sense of national identity.

Homi's father, Jehangir, an Oxford-educated individual who commenced his career in Mysore's judicial service, later became a legal adviser to the House of Tatas, fostering his own interests in Western classical music, painting, and botanical pursuits. Jehangir's involvement in the Tata companies and his appreciation for arts and culture significantly influenced Homi's upbringing. Their home was more than just a place of residence; it was a centre of learning and cultural richness that moulded Homi's cosmopolitan outlook.

The Bhabha family's lineage and connections were not insignificant in shaping Homi's trajectory. His mother, Meherbai Panday, belonged to a respected family. Her father, Sir Dinshaw Petit, was known for his philanthropic endeavours in Bombay. Meherbai's premature passing deeply impacted the family, and her father laid the foundation for a school in her honour, which Homi later held in high regard.

The family's ties extended to the Tatas through marriage. Homi's paternal aunt, Meherbai Bhabha, commonly known as Mehri, was married to Sir Dorabji Tata, the elder son of Jamsetji Tata. The union was a strategic one, seemingly arranged by Jamsetji, who thought highly of the Bhabha family. Mehri's marriage to Dorabji Tata, facilitated by a seemingly casual meeting orchestrated by Jamsetji, had long-reaching implications for Homi's adult life.

The accounts of family connections, marriages, and strategic introductions shed light on the interwoven relationships within influential circles that eventually played a role in shaping Homi's life and positioning him within influential circles as he grew into adulthood.

Homi Jehangir Bhabha's family connections within the prominent industrial circles of Bombay and their familiarity with the Parsi culture of philanthropy played a pivotal role in setting the stage for his later endeavours in institution-building. The support and ties within these networks, particularly with the Tatas, were instrumental in shaping his path and garnering support for his future initiatives.

Jehangir and Meherbai Bhabha, after their marriage, established a rich home environment in Bombay, marked by a diverse collection of books that encompassed literature, arts, sciences, and technical subjects. This extensive library, a joint effort of Hormusji, Jehangir, and Meherbai, reflected their intellectual pursuits and evolving interests. It was not only a hub for knowledge but also a nurturing ground for young Homi's growing talents in mathematics and sciences. Their home also boasted a garden and canine companions, creating a congenial environment that fostered Homi's intellectual and artistic interests from an early age.

As a child, Homi's sleeplessness concerned his family, leading them to seek medical advice during a trip to Europe in 1913. In Paris, they consulted a renowned paediatrician who was captivated by the young Bhabha's active mind. With an intuitive foresight, the doctor reassured the parents that all their son required was a conducive environment to flourish into a genius, attributing Homi's sleeplessness to his extraordinarily active brain.

The Bhabha household was characterised by more than just an intellectually stimulating environment. Jamshed, Homi's younger brother, fondly reminisced about their parents' happy marriage and the overall positive atmosphere in their upbringing. He emphasised the significance of a stress-free and supportive environment for their development. The siblings shared a close bond, with Jamshed regarding Homi not just as a brother but also as a nurturing figure, akin to a second father.

However, there are varying perspectives on the relationship between the Bhabha brothers. While some portray Jamshed as harbouring feelings of jealousy toward Homi's success and standing within the ruling establishment, others recount a more affectionate and respectful bond between the siblings. Reports differ on how openly Jamshed spoke of his elder brother after Homi's demise, suggesting potential unspoken sentiments or differing perceptions regarding their relationship within Tata circles.

These differing accounts shed light on the complexities and nuances within the fraternal relationship, leaving room for varied interpretations and perceptions among those who observed or were associated with the brothers.

Homi Jehangir Bhabha, known for his contributions to science and nuclear research, had an enduring bond with his parents, particularly his mother, Meherbai. After his father's passing in 1942, Homi expressed his profound affection for both his parents in letters to notable figures in the scientific community. However, it was his mother, Meherbai, who remained a constant emotional pillar in his life. Homi ensured to take her on vacations every summer, displaying a strong devotion to her. Meherbai, even in her later years, maintained a dignified appearance, impeccably dressed in a white silk sari and Victorian blouse adorned with pearls, diamonds, and fashionable leather shoes from abroad.

Their relationship was marked by a unique language, a blend of English and Parsi-Gujarati, which added a distinct charm to their communication. Despite her elegance and grace, Meherbai was affectionately given the nickname "Twit" by Homi, a term of endearment that held special significance between them.

During his formative years at the Cathedral and John Connon Boys' School in Bombay, Homi had the privilege of being in close proximity to Esplanade House, the opulent residence of Jamsetji Tata. He often had his meals and spent valuable hours in the extensive library at the Tata residence, in addition to their family's own collection of books. Meherbai Tata, his aunt, and Sir Dorabji Tata provided affection akin to that of parents to the Bhabha brothers, nurturing Homi's intellectual curiosity.

Meherbai Tata, Homi's aunt, was a remarkable personality herself. Not only a prominent tennis player who attracted attention by playing in saris and representing India at the Paris Olympics in 1924, she was also a frequent participant at Wimbledon. Her varied talents extended to being an accomplished pianist sought after for public concerts in Mysore. Furthermore, she owned the notable Jubilee diamond, a remarkable 245.35-carat gem, ranked as the sixth largest diamond in the world. Meherbai actively engaged in charitable endeavours, contributing significantly during the First World War and being honoured as a Commander of the British Empire by King George V for her service to the Indian Red Cross society.

The dynamic and accomplished women in Homi's family, particularly his mother and aunt, played integral roles in not just shaping his familial relationships but also in influencing his perspective and approach to life and success.

Homi Jehangir Bhabha's formative years were shaped by the familial and socio-political environment that encompassed nationalistic influences and pivotal interactions with eminent figures. His mother, Meherbai, a staunch advocate for women's emancipation, was deeply involved in the advocacy and enactment of pivotal legislation such as the Child Marriage Restraint Act, 1929, and was a vocal proponent for women's suffrage, girls' education, and the elimination of the purdah system in India. Unfortunately, Meherbai passed away in 1931 in Wales, leaving a void in Bhabha's life.

Bhabha's proximity to influential figures within India's industrial and political landscape was instrumental in shaping his worldview. His close association with the Tatas provided him with first-hand exposure to significant nationalist movements and key leaders. He was privy to discussions on national issues, economic development, and the establishment of industries, offering him a unique perspective on adaptive strategies and relationships between foreign firms and Indian leaders.

At the age of 18, Bhabha went abroad, equipped with a profound understanding of how his community navigated the tumultuous political climate and excelled in a colonial situation. Such exposure to foreign leaders and nationalist politicians influenced his broad vision and strategic understanding within both national and international contexts. He acquired an astute ability to plan and organise, a rarity among scientists who often remain focused within narrow academic or research spheres.

His early intellectual prowess was evident as he delved into Einstein's Special Theory of Relativity, an achievement quite remarkable for someone of his age at that time. Bhabha's capacity to think abstractly and understand the limitations of perceiving the natural world solely through ordinary senses distinguished him, propelling him to a unique level of scientific insight.

Homi Jehangir Bhabha excelled academically, receiving honours and recognition during his schooling and thereafter. His remarkable achievements and his subsequent ascension to a prominent position in the scientific community were acknowledged and admired by his former headmaster, CH Hammond, who expressed pride in having played a small role in Bhabha's education.

His journey toward higher education led him through Elphinstone College and the Royal Institute of Science before he ventured to Cambridge University. His experiences at the Royal Institute, where he encountered the concept of cosmic rays from Compton, were deeply formative, setting the stage for his future academic pursuits in Cambridge.

As Compton won the Nobel Prize for his ground-breaking discoveries in physics, Bhabha set sail for Cambridge University to pursue Mechanical Sciences, embarking on a fascinating academic journey that meandered through mechanical engineering, mathematics, theoretical physics, and beyond. This phase marked the initiation of an illustrious scientific career that would eventually solidify his legacy in the field of nuclear research and theoretical physics.

*****

Cambridge wasn't just an educational institution; it was a capital of knowledge. Comprising about 30 self-governing colleges, each led by a master and staffed by esteemed fellows who held university lecturer or professor positions, it stood as a pinnacle of academic excellence. Each college was responsible for selecting its own undergraduates and overseeing their academic and social needs. The college education system involved close tutelage, almost akin to parental supervision, covering students' general welfare and academic progress, in addition to structured programmes of study, lectures, and examinations organised by the university.

One of the notable colleges within the Cambridge network was Gonville and Caius, where Bhabha was admitted. The college, with its dual name, had a rich history, founded in 1384 and then again in 1557. Students entering this college passed through three gates: Humilitatis, Virtutis, and the Gate of Honour. The Gate of Honour held particular significance, marking a key academic rite of passage. Students would pass through it to collect their degrees, making it a symbol of achievement. Another notable occasion for the opening of this gate was to mark the fellow student's death. Bhabha's choice of this college was influenced by the fact that his uncle, Sir Dorabji Tata, was an alumnus and a generous patron, making significant donations to the college in 1920. Dorabji, however, had to cut short his studies and return to India in 1879 after just two years due to familial circumstances, being recalled by his grandfather, Nusserwanji Tata, who couldn't bear to be separated from him any longer. Upon arriving at Cambridge in 1927, Bhabha pursued BA in mechanical engineering, aligning with the hopes of both his father and uncle, who aspired for him to return to India after completing his degree and contribute to the House of Tatas.

The expectation of pursuing a career in pure science during that time, especially in the colonies, was seen as unrealistic, as opportunities in engineering, particularly in projects like the steel works at Jamshedpur, held more pragmatic promise. However, Bhabha had a different vision. Despite having a talent for mechanical drawings and understanding engineering well, he was not inspired by the field. His correspondence with Homi Seervai, a noted constitutional jurist, revealed his deep discontent with engineering. In fact, there were times when he expressed not just dislike but even contempt and hatred for the subject.

Homi Seervai, who gained fame later in life for his significant contributions to constitutional law and his pivotal role in the Kesavananda Bharti case, received a letter from Bhabha on 2nd August 1928. In this correspondence, Bhabha candidly expressed his dissatisfaction with his current syllabus, stating vehemently that his true passion lay in physics and astrophysics. He made it clear that nothing would deter him from pursuing these fields. Furthermore, he emphatically stated that he had no interest in joining the steel industry back in India, a decision that would later shape his exceptional journey in the realm of science and theoretical physics.

Aside from the fact that he did not delve much into his personal matters, there were numerous distractions for a young man in the academic hub of Cambridge. He enthusiastically immersed himself in extracurricular activities and sports. Enjoying the charm of Cambridge, he often partook in delightful activities like Cam, Sunday picnics by the riverbank and leisurely afternoon teas.

His days were filled with supervisions, where small groups of two to four students received instruction. Evenings were no less busy, as Bhabha would frequently stroll along the Cam or go for a run at the university cricket ground, known as "fanners." Moreover, there were countless parties to attend, adding to the vibrant social scene that he thoroughly enjoyed.

Bhabha had a deep passion for Western classical music and spent time comprehending its composition and structure. He even tried his hand at composing some pieces. In his letters to friends and family, he shared his dedication to understanding musical intricacies, such as studying counterpoints for an hour daily. He vividly recounted his experience of witnessing Beethoven's ninth Symphony performance in London during November 1927, which left an indelible mark on him.

Bhabha also developed a newfound passion for coxing during the boat races at Cambridge. Coxing involved taking a position at the stern, facing the rowers, and assuming the responsibility of guiding and steering them through the straightest course. In this role, he not only had to provide navigation but also lead, motivate, and exhort the rowers to strive for a victorious finish. It was a dynamic role that allowed him to actively contribute to the team's success by providing both strategic direction and encouragement to the rowers.

Years later, when MGK Menon asked Bhabha why he chose science as a career over the arts, he responded that while the arts made life fulfilling, he aspired to pursue science as a profession. He believed in contributing to the understanding of the world through science.

Art critic Rudolf von Leyden, a close associate of Bhabha during the 1940s and 1950s in Bombay, observed that Dr. Bhabha strongly felt that the cerebral scientist needed to find a counterpart in the sensory experiences of the arts. Bhabha's activities at Cambridge served as strong evidence of this idea. He engaged in artistic pursuits, including painting and sketching from models, often in a romantic symbolist style. Furthermore, he delved into experimenting intensively with abstract visual interpretations of musical themes, drawing upon his profound knowledge of the mathematical structure of music. This approach underscored his conviction that the intellectual scientist needed to complement the sensory engagement found in the arts, portraying a holistic understanding of the human experience.

Shortly after arriving in Cambridge, Bhabha expressed to his father his burgeoning interest in physics and his lack of enthusiasm for mechanical engineering. The first part of the tripos results proved disappointing as he secured a third class, much to his father's distress. In response, his father issued an ultimatum: attain a first class in the second part or face a recall to India. Bhabha skilfully negotiated, promising the desired first class if his father would sponsor two more years for him to delve into mathematical studies.

What Bhabha wrote in an emotional letter to his father from Cambridge shows how determined and forward-thinking a future scientist needs to be. When he wrote these words in 1928, he had a deep understanding of who he was and what he wanted. Bhabha made it clear that a job in business or engineering was not in line with who he was and was very different from his personality and views. He thought that math was his true calling and the way to become a great person. He was sure that everyone is best at what they are deeply interested in and what matches their real skills. This was a belief he held for himself in the field of physics.

In the message, Bhabha talked about his goals and passion for physics and how much he wanted to study it. He said that his success would be measured by how hard he worked and what he did in the field of physics, not by what other people thought. Bhabha was also very aware of the promise of science in India. He disagreed with the idea that India was a country that couldn't make scientific progress.

His words made it clear that physics was the only thing he wanted to do, because they showed how much he wanted to learn about it. He didn't want to be successful in the usual ways or be in charge of a big company. Bhabha understood that other people might choose different paths, like running a successful business, but he knew that science was his true calling.

In his plea to his father, Bhabha talked about the nature of goals and how it is impossible to tell someone what road to take. He used famous people like Berlioz and Beethoven as examples to show that a person's calling is highly personal and can't be forced by other people's opinions or expectations. In the end, he sincerely asked his father to back his interest in physics, stressing how important and urgent it was to him.

His growing obsession with mathematics and physics was apparent in his letters, where he vehemently criticised engineering, deeming it beneath his intellect. He believed engineering was a mundane field for those with average intelligence, a sentiment he did not shy away from expressing. Prior to his examination, he conveyed to his father a lasting statement - that exams do not truly measure original or creative abilities. Yet, he assured his father that he would achieve the desired results, securing a first class in the mechanical tripos.

In 1930, Bhabha's father honoured his promise, enabling Bhabha's admission to the mathematical tripos at Cambridge. His passion for mathematics can be understood in the context of its significant influence on the development of mathematical physics in England during that time. Physics was taught as part of the mathematical tripos, and for Bhabha, it was a pathway to engage with the great creative minds of the West. Unlike mechanical engineering, which he saw as limited and mundane, physics allowed Bhabha to ponder the profound mysteries of existence.

Ultimately, his decision to switch to physics marked a pivotal moment. It was through this transition that the young aristocrat found his professional calling.

How science was at the time is a key part of knowing what drew young Homi Bhabha to the field of physics. During this time, Cambridge was a place where many important science discoveries were made.

JJ Thompson found the electron in 1897 at the well-known Cavendish Laboratory in Cambridge. This was a big step forward. This finding caused a big change in physics and opened the door to new questions and ideas. Soon after, in 1910, Ernest Rutherford moved to Cambridge, which led to the discovery of the atomic nucleus and a challenge to traditional physics.

Rutherford's results went against classical physics, which said that electrons circling a positively charged nucleus would lose energy and fall into the nucleus over time. This meant that scientists had to change the way they think. At the same time, Albert Einstein's Special Theory of Relativity, which came out in the first ten years of the 20th century, threw out old ideas about space, time, and movement. It showed that distances and times are relative and change for people who are moving.

Einstein's theory of relativity had a big effect on physics. It included the effects of gravity and made the theory work for people moving at high speeds. Einstein's ground-breaking idea that light bends near large objects was proven correct by an experiment during a solar eclipse in 1919.

At the same time, it was figured out that light is both a wave and a particle. Radiation spectra experiments showed that light behaves like a particle. Einstein added to this idea by suggesting that light is made up of particles and showing how light could move electrons out of metals.

In addition to all this, Rutherford's studies led to Niels Bohr's ground-breaking atomic model in 1913. This model introduced the idea of energy quantisation for electrons inside atoms. Electrons were now limited to certain levels of energy, and when they moved between these levels, they gave off or took in individual "packets of light" called photons. This was a big change from traditional physics because it brought in the idea of "quanta."

In the early 1920s, a new theory called quantum physics was created to explain how particles behave at the atomic and molecular levels. The rules of quantum physics were made by people with big ideas, like Erwin Schrödinger and Werner Heisenberg. Wolfgang Pauli came up with the exclusion principle, which says that no two electrons can be in the same state. This laid the groundwork for knowing how the elements in the periodic table behave.

Heisenberg's uncertainty principle, which he came up with in 1927, was another big discovery. It questioned the idea that you could precisely measure the position and speed of a particle in the atomic world at the same time. It said that such exact measurements have a natural limit.

In the same year, Paul Dirac tried to bring together Einstein's theory of special relativity and quantum physics in his work at Cambridge. This led to the idea of a "Dirac sea" of electrons with negative energy, which led to the prediction of "positrons," which were later found in cosmic rays in 1932.

Scientists were excited to apply these new ideas to molecules and even chemistry because of the success of quantum physics in explaining the features of atoms. The quantum revolution was changing the way physics and chemistry were done. It captivated the scientific community and marked a turning point in history, which Homi Bhabha would soon be a part of as he began his career in science.

At about the same time, Satyendra Nath Bose, a young scientist from Dhaka University, came up with a new way to use statistical methods to calculate light as particles. Louis de Broglie also thought that matter could behave like a wave in certain situations. This theory added to the growing understanding of quantum physics.

As Homi Bhabha arrived in Cambridge during a period of significant advancements in physics, particularly in the realm of quantum mechanics and atomic theory, it was indeed a propitious time for him to pursue his burgeoning passion for physics.

Having been captivated by the subject during his school years and inspired by the illuminating public lecture by Compton in Bombay, the allure of engaging in cutting-edge physics research at a prestigious institution like Cambridge was irresistible.

Cambridge was a vibrant hub of scientific exploration, attracting brilliant minds from around the world who were pushing the boundaries of existing scientific knowledge. The revolutionary ideas and discoveries in physics during this era were fundamentally altering the way the universe was understood, and Bhabha was in the midst of it all.

Given his deep-rooted fascination with the mysteries of the physical world, it was a natural progression for Bhabha to delve into research and contribute to this dynamic field. The intellectual atmosphere and the unfolding scientific paradigm in Cambridge perfectly aligned with Bhabha's aspirations and provided him with the ideal environment to explore and immerse himself in the captivating realm of physics.

Rising Like A 'Balloon'

Cosmic rays are high-energy particles, mostly protons and atomic nuclei, originating from sources outside Earth's atmosphere, likely from various astrophysical processes such as supernovae, black holes, or active galactic nuclei. These energetic particles continuously bombard the Earth from outer space. While the term "rays" may suggest radiation, cosmic rays are actually composed of various charged particles, including electrons, positrons, and atomic nuclei.

The discovery of cosmic rays began with Victor Hess's balloon experiments in the early 20th century, where he observed an increase in radiation levels at higher altitudes, leading to the term "cosmic rays." These rays pose potential health risks to astronauts because in space, beyond Earth's protective atmosphere, they are exposed to these high-energy particles, which can cause cellular damage.

The study of cosmic rays has significantly contributed to the field of high-energy physics. Before the advent of large particle accelerators, cosmic rays were the primary source of high-energy particles for experimentation. When these energetic cosmic particles collide with molecules in the atmosphere, they create showers of secondary particles, providing a natural laboratory to study particle interactions.

There are distinctions within cosmic rays, classified as "soft" and "hard" components based on their energy levels. The "soft" component can be stopped by a few millimetres of lead, while the "hard" component can penetrate several metres of lead, highlighting the disparity in their energy levels.

Early observations revealed that these cosmic rays sometimes arrive in "showers" of particles spread out in space. Further experiments using cloud chambers demonstrated that when a high-energy particle interacts with matter, it can produce a spray of secondary particles, akin to a billiard ball transforming into multiple balls upon impact. This phenomenon illustrates how the energy of the incoming particle can transform into the masses of new particles, as per Einstein's famous equation $E=mc^2$, which shows the equivalence of mass and energy.

The origins of cosmic rays and the mechanisms by which they attain such high energies remain areas of active research and exploration in astrophysics and particle physics. Studying these particles provides valuable insights into the fundamental nature of matter, energy, and the universe's workings.

At the time when only a handful of particles—such as the electron, proton, and neutron (discovered in 1932 at the Cavendish laboratory in Cambridge)—were known, the process of particle multiplication was challenging to explain. Understanding the phenomenon of showers required additional particles. The recently discovered positrons seemed a potential solution, leading Bhabha to investigate the roles of electrons and positrons in these cascading events.

Bhabha made a significant decision to focus on cosmic rays for his PhD, a choice that intriguingly developed into one of his lifelong passions. His selection was purposeful as it offered him the opportunity to investigate various aspects, including the testing of Dirac's theory on the sea of negative energy states of the electron.

The year 1932 marked a pivotal period at the Cavendish laboratory, famously termed the 'annus mirabilis', witnessing ground-breaking discoveries like the positron and neutron. This year coincided with Bhabha's collaboration with Fowler, initiating his work on cosmic rays. Engulfed in the excitement of these new findings, Bhabha was in the right place at the right time, as many later observed.

Before starting his doctoral research, Bhabha had already encountered cosmic rays during a visit to India by Compton, whose primary objective was to measure a specific property of cosmic rays across the globe. Bhabha's initial scientific contribution was a paper concerning the interaction of cosmic rays with Earth's atmosphere, reflecting his early involvement and interest in this area of study.

In 1932, Bhabha embarked on a journey through Europe under a Rouse Ball Travelling Studentship. During this period, he collaborated with notable physicists such as Wolfgang Pauli in Zurich, Enrico Fermi in Rome, and Hendrik Kramers in Utrecht. It was during his visit to Zurich in 1933 that he authored his maiden scientific paper, 'Zur Absorption der Hohenstrahlung' (Absorption of cosmic rays), which was subsequently published in Zeitschrift Fur Physik.

His paper delved into the behaviour of highly energetic gamma rays, a type of high-energy photons, upon entering Earth's atmosphere. When these gamma rays collide with atmospheric nuclei, they generate an electron and a positron pair. These particles interact within the air, continuously losing energy as they interact with the surrounding air molecules, emitting photons themselves. If these newly generated photons possess enough energy, they, too, create electron-positron pairs, continuing this chain reaction until the resulting photons lack the necessary energy to generate further pairs. At this point, the original gamma ray photon is considered absorbed by the atmosphere. Essentially, this results in a cascading effect, a series of showers involving electrons and positrons originating from a gamma ray photon until its absorption. This process was visually captured in 1932 at the Cavendish laboratory, marking yet another achievement during their renowned 'annus mirabilis'.

In the Cavendish laboratory, through an experiment using a chamber saturated with vapour, the trajectory of particles created after a collision with a gamma ray photon left a visible trail in the form of a cloud. Patrick Blackett and Giuseppe Occhialini successfully captured the process of pair production by a gamma ray photon for the first time. Bhabha's debut scientific paper focused on the theoretical calculation of this phenomenon, an accomplishment that earned him the Isaac Newton Studentship in 1934.

During his time at Enrico Fermi's laboratory in Rome, Bhabha delved deeper into the process he had been exploring. In 1933, Fermi and George Uhlenbeck proposed a theory stating that an incident photon initially generates an electron-positron pair. Following this, the positron sheds some of its energy through collisions. Eventually, the positron could either unite with a free electron, resulting in the creation of two low-energy photons, or it could combine with an electron confined within an atom, leading to the generation of a high-energy photon. Despite Fermi's efforts to estimate the likelihood of these interactions, the calculated probabilities did not align with experimental findings.

Motivated to approach the problem from the perspective of Dirac's sea of negative energy electrons, Bhabha collaborated with HR Hulme from his alma mater, Cambridge, to develop an innovative methodology for computing the rates of these two distinct interactions. Although their results did not substantially clarify the experimental disparities, the approach they devised was notably pioneering. Their joint paper, detailing this new method, was published in the Proceedings of the Royal Society in 1934, contributing to Bhabha earning his PhD in 1935.

Subsequently, Bhabha redirected his focus to exploring the interaction between a fast, charged particle and the eventual creation of an electron-positron pair. This analysis was intricate due to the numerous potential pathways this process could take, necessitating the consideration of all possibilities. In retrospect, it becomes apparent that these investigations were steering Bhabha toward formulating a comprehensive theory concerning air showers generated by cosmic rays.

Shortly thereafter, Bhabha embarked on what would become his pivotal contribution, now famously recognised in textbooks as the 'Bhabha scattering' process. This involved examining the interaction between an electron and a positron. When these particles interact, one observes the resultant outgoing electron and positron. In the realm of quantum mechanics, an intriguing principle is that two electrons are indistinguishable from each other, being treated as identical entities. Consequently, the outgoing particles might either be entirely new or the same as the incoming particles. In one scenario, the incoming particles could 'annihilate', briefly generating a gamma ray photon, which, in turn, gives rise to a new pair of an electron and a positron. Alternatively, the incoming and outgoing particles may interact via their electric fields, resulting in scattering away (where a 'virtual' photon is involved in quantum mechanical terms).

The magnitude of this interaction hinges on both possibilities, leading Bhabha to undertake a complex and crucial calculation. While prior work had been done on electron scattering off another electron by Mott in 1929, demonstrating the significant role of indistinguishability, it was uncertain whether the same principles held for electron-positron scattering. Bhabha's paper titled 'The scattering of positrons by electrons with exchange on Dirac's theory of positrons' was published in 1936 in the Proceedings of the Royal Society. Experimental confirmation finally emerged in 1954, aligning remarkably well with Bhabha's predictions. Presently, modern experimental facilities for high-energy particle interactions are often calibrated by initially conducting electron-positron scattering experiments and validating the results against Bhabha's theoretical predictions.

At the young age of 27, Bhabha achieved a significant milestone with the publication of the pivotal paper. He continued his research, collaborating with Walter Heitler, who was then based in Bristol, on developing a theory concerning electron showers in the atmosphere. Together, they revisited the process of generating a cascade of particles akin to an avalanche in the atmosphere. Despite the collective efforts of several physicists, understanding the mechanism behind these showers remained an enigma. Even luminaries such as Heisenberg had speculated on the process, suggesting that the incoming particle might trigger a massive explosion upon colliding with an atmospheric nucleus, resulting in the observed particles as mere debris of this explosion.

Hans Bethe, later a Nobel Prize recipient for his work on nuclear reactions within stars, had partnered with Heitler for an initial calculation of this cascade process. Their fundamental query involved predicting the quantity of electrons at a certain depth below the top layer of the atmosphere if a specific number of electrons with particular energy levels entered the top layer. According to Bethe and Heitler, fast, energetic electrons should be obstructed by a 2-km thick atmospheric layer. This, however, posed a quandary as the number of fast electrons observed at sea level was notably large. The discrepancy arose: if the incoming cosmic rays were halted by the upper atmosphere, then what accounted for the abundance of fast electrons at sea level? Conversely, if the observed sea level electrons originated in cascading showers, then there appeared to be an inconsistency with the Bethe-Heitler calculations.

The crux of the issue lay in computing the radiation energy loss of electrons in the atmosphere. Moreover, there was a growing apprehension regarding the viability of the standard theory of quantum electrodynamics at these high-energy levels, hinting at a potential breakdown in its applicability.

Bhabha and Heitler embarked on a fresh calculation, and with their detailed and comprehensive theory, they determined that the atmosphere's stopping power had been previously overestimated. Instead of a 2 km thickness, it would require about 8 km of the atmosphere to halt the fast electrons. Consequently, they successfully accounted for the observed quantity of fast electrons at sea level within the framework of standard quantum electrodynamics. Moreover, their findings dismissed Heisenberg's notion of an explosion hypothesis, which would have restricted the number of fast electrons reaching sea level if they were merely remnants of a singular large-scale explosion in the upper atmosphere.

Heitler reminisced about their collaborative work, remarking, "It [the idea for the cascade process] must have been 'in the air,' and I am sure several physicists thought about it. We soon found ourselves, Bhabha and I, calculating what should, according to the theory, happen step-by-step when a fast electron passes through matter, the emission of several gamma-quanta, each of which would subsequently create a pair, which in turn would emit gamma-quanta, which again create pairs and so on till the energy was exhausted. This was the theory of showers" (from 'Bhabha and his Magnificent Obsessions').

Meanwhile, across the Atlantic, J Robert Oppenheimer and JF Carlson were also engaged in similar research. Their paper was received by the Physical Review on December 8, 1936, while Bhabha and Heitler's paper reached the Royal Society on December 11. Both papers arrived at similar conclusions and methodologies, albeit with some minor differences. Bhabha's work began to gain attention, leading to his receipt of the 1851

Exhibition Scholarship in 1937, enabling him to continue his research at Cambridge.

The Bhabha–Heitler calculation addressed the 'soft' segment of cosmic rays, a realm compatible with the established Dirac's theory of positrons. Bhabha then redirected his focus towards the 'hard' section, which displayed higher energy levels and increased penetration in cosmic rays. This particular portion notably lacked electrons, leading Bhabha, through insightful intuition, to suggest the existence of unknown particles. In an October 1937 paper analysing cosmic rays, Bhabha proposed that a significant portion of the 'hard' component consisted of particles approximately a hundred times more massive than electrons.

This conjecture was remarkably bold for its time, reflecting Bhabha's confidence even at the age of 28. At a weekend conference in Manchester, Patrick Blackett, then 39 and a future Nobel laureate, contended that the quantum theory of radiation might face challenges at high energies, asserting that there couldn't be particles heavier than electrons in the 'hard' segment of cosmic rays. Despite opposition, Bhabha persisted in proposing the involvement of a more substantial particle. Initially challenged during the meeting, Blackett hesitated to acknowledge the possibility of error. However, within a few months, he conceded, and in 1938, Bhabha was recognised with the Adams Prize in physics for his contributions.

Bhabha's suggestion implied that these particles fell within the mass range between electrons and protons, prompting the question: What could these particles be? And the answers were nowhere to be found.

Two years prior to Bhabha's paper, Japanese physicist Hideki Yukawa postulated a distinct force holding the nucleus together, a force differing from electromagnetic and gravitational forces known to physicists. It needed to counteract the mutual repulsion of positively charged protons, operating within a short range and exclusively inside the nucleus. Yukawa proposed that a massive particle could limit a force's range, estimating the mediator particle for the 'strong force' to be several hundred times more massive than an electron. Learning of Yukawa's work, Bhabha authored a 1938 paper introducing the 'heavy electron,' developed a theory on nuclear forces, and considered Einstein's theory of relativity's application to these particles, predicting their decay patterns due to time dilation effects.

Carl David Anderson coined the term 'mesotron' for this new particle, but Bhabha preferred 'meson.' He argued for this term's logic and brevity in a 1939 Nature paper, cementing its usage. However, it emerged that there were two distinct particles involved: the pi-meson (pion), as predicted by Yukawa for the strong force, and the mu-meson (muon), heavier than the electron, associated with the hard cosmic ray component. Indian physicists Debendra Mohan Bose and Bibha Choudhury conducted an experiment in the Darjeeling hills, detecting evidence of both pions and muons, though their findings weren't initially acknowledged.

Bhabha's predictions on time dilation effects, crucial for muon decay, were integral to understanding observed muon behaviour but often overlooked in textbooks. His insights presented the first experimental test of Einstein's prediction. Simultaneously, Bhabha delved into theoretical aspects of mesons, earning praise from the physics community.

Amid his scientific pursuits, Bhabha maintained his artistic inclinations, exemplified by a painted portrait gifted at a Cavendish laboratory dinner. He also became involved in political and social ideologies, joining the Socialist Club and being influenced by JD Bernal's belief in the societal impact of science. Bernalism advocated for a structured scientific approach to address global issues in independent nations, likely shaping Bhabha's futuristic views on science and technology in post-colonial India.

Bhabha gained recognition among his peers, leading to an invitation to join the Kapitza Club—an exclusive gathering of physicists that convened informally in the 1920s and 1930s at Cambridge. Initiated by the esteemed Russian scientist Pyotr Leonidovich Kapitza, who was a favourite of Rutherford, the club sought to defy the rigid hierarchies prevalent in British physics education. Kapitza, known for his multilingual but humorous and engaging persona, established the club in reaction to what he perceived as excessive deference among British physics students towards their elders and the overly structured environment at Cambridge.

The Kapitza Club's ethos centred around a weekly seminar focusing on cutting-edge physics discussions, disregarding traditional academic rankings. Membership was exclusive and attainable only by presenting a talk, with the strict rule that missing several meetings led to withdrawal of membership. The gatherings took place in Kapitza's Trinity College room on Tuesday evenings, featuring volunteer speakers utilising chalk and blackboards for presentations. Notably, Kapitza deliberately introduced errors into discussions to encourage participation, allowing even the most junior members to correct him and break away from conventional thinking.

Bhabha presented on the "heavy electron" in February 1938, an event later acknowledged by Cockroft in his memoir. The significance of being part of this elite group extended beyond scientific discourse. Bhabha's interactions with some of the finest minds in the field proved invaluable in his future role as an institution builder and science organiser.

Kapitza departed from Cambridge in 1934 due to Soviet authorities preventing his return, taking along his original equipment used in high magnetic field experiments at the Mont Laboratory in Cambridge. Rumours persist that ground-breaking scientific revelations were informally revealed during these club meetings. For instance, it's said that James Chadwick first announced his results within the Kapitza Club's gathering.

The club's activities ceased in 1958 but was revived in 1966 when Kapitza, after more than two decades, was permitted to visit Cambridge. This reunion allowed the surviving members, including Dirac and Cockcroft, to convene for one final meeting, where they reminisced over fine wine, a stark contrast to the past meetings where only basic coffee was available. The gathering marked the official end of an era for this historically significant and influential scientific club.

Another notable event occurred at the Cavendish Laboratory, which had a longstanding tradition of hosting an annual dinner organised by its students. The last such pre-Second World War dinner took place on 19 December 1938. The guest of honour was Herbert Austin, the first Baron Austin, who had generously announced a major benefaction in 1936 to build what became known as the Austin Wing of the Cavendish Laboratory. Sir Maurice Vincent Wilkes, a distinguished British computer scientist, recollects Bhabha's involvement during this dinner, highlighting the significance of this occasion for the young physicist.

Bhabha seized this opportunity to showcase his high spirits and distinctive talents. His most striking contribution was a full-sized portrait of Lord Austin, painted by Bhabha himself. This portrait was ceremoniously presented to Lord Austin during the dinner, reportedly painted on brown paper. Wilkes also recalled another playful gesture during the same evening, which he believed stemmed from Bhabha's mischievous spirit.

The playful episode involved a linguistic pun on the term "wing," which has dual meanings in English. Apart from being an architectural feature, it is also a term used to describe a part of an Austin car—fittingly coinciding with Lord Austin's association with the construction of the Austin Wing at the laboratory. As a humorous gesture, a wing from an old Austin Seven car, duly painted, was presented to Lord Austin during the dinner. The reaction of Lord Austin to this unconventional gift remains unknown. The slightly damaged painting that was presented to him is currently stored in the museum section of the laboratory.

Additionally, another significant figure, an Indian named Rappal Sangameshwaran Krishnan, a protégé of Raman, was present at Cambridge during this time. It is speculated that this dinner might have marked Krishnan's first encounter with Bhabha. Notably, the construction of the new building, the Austin Wing, was completed in 1940. However, due to the war, its use was delayed, and it was eventually handed back to the university in 1945.

The Austin Wing went on to witness ground-breaking scientific discoveries, including the elucidation of the structure of DNA by Francis H.C. Crick, James D. Watson, and Maurice H.F. Wilkins. This monumental discovery led to the joint awarding of the Nobel Prize in Medicine in 1962 to these eminent scientists for their remarkable contributions.

Blackett extended an offer for Bhabha to join the faculty at Manchester, but prior to this opportunity, Bhabha left England in the summer of 1939 for a holiday in India. However, before departing, he met KS Krishnan in Cambridge in June of that year. Their introduction had been facilitated by Chandrasekhar, and the three Indian scientists shared a memorable lunch together on June 22, 1939.

Krishnan and Bhabha's relationship deepened over time. They later collaborated on the Atomic Energy Commission (AEC) and developed a strong friendship. Years down the line, Bhabha visited Krishnan at his home in New Delhi, where they enjoyed a traditional South Indian dinner while the soothing sounds of Carnatic music played in the background, emanating from the latest tape recorder.

The outbreak of the Second World War in September 1939, however, altered Bhabha's plans. Stranded in India due to the war's onset, he had to recalibrate his career path in unfamiliar territory. Despite the challenges, he managed to flourish and make significant contributions, underscoring an essential phase in his life story.

Bhabha's scientific research during his time at Cambridge was distinguished by its exceptional quality. Although not marked by a single innovative discovery akin to Einstein, his contributions were pivotal and substantial. His legacy wasn't to be defined by a singular event but by his consistent, dedicated work within his field, marking him as a physicist of significance.

Notably, Bhabha's career coincided with India's quest for independence, and his efforts aligned with the nation's endeavours to leverage science and technology in service of the country. Bhabha, an adept administrator, played a crucial role in orchestrating and implementing initiatives that achieved considerable success in the scientific realm. Consequently, he is remembered more for his administrative prowess and contributions to the scientific infrastructure, even though his earlier scientific contributions were of the highest order.

While Bhabha was nominated for the Nobel Prize in Physics on five occasions, he never secured the prize himself. However, he experienced better fortune in being a nominator for the prize, signifying the respect and recognition he garnered within the scientific community.

❑

Struggling to Go Back or a New Beginning?

Bhabha's arrival in India during the summer of 1939, a customary visit for his annual vacation, took an unexpected turn due to the outbreak of World War II in September of that year. Initially, Bhabha intended to return to England after a few months, yet the global conflict and various circumstances prompted a significant change in his plans. The prevailing conditions in England and the worldwide scientific community, which heavily engaged in the war efforts, shifted Bhabha's perspective on his return.

The landscape in England had transformed, with most scientists prioritising contributions to the war rather than pursuing fundamental research. Consequently, the prospect of returning to England lost its allure, leading Bhabha to postpone his departure, anticipating a swift end to the war, at least for the following six months.

Known for his proactive nature, Bhabha began reaching out to physicists in India. During this time, an opportunity arose at the Indian Institute of Science (IISc) in Bangalore, courtesy of CV Raman. Bhabha embraced this offer. However, his transition to IISc occurred amid a tumultuous period for the institution. Internal conflicts marred the environment, primarily characterised by discord between the governing council and CV Raman, the institute's first Indian director.

The discord had escalated to the point where Raman was relieved of his directorial responsibilities and relegated to a mere professorship within the physics department in 1937—two years prior to Bhabha's arrival. This context sets the stage for Bhabha's entry into a setting marked by internal tensions and a shifting institutional landscape at the Indian Institute of Science.

In 1940, Bhabha commenced his journey at the Indian Institute of Science (IISc) with a readership position in the physics department. During this period, his affiliation was noted as 'at present at IISc' in various papers, including a publication in Nature in March 1940. Bhabha used this time to present a series of 25 lectures focusing on his research on cosmic rays. Initially, his appointment was for six months, but due to the Tata Trusts' request, it was extended for an additional five months.

To support Bhabha's scientific endeavours at IISc, the Sir Dorab Tata Trust provided him with a grant. This financial assistance aided in establishing Bhabha's cosmic ray research unit. Notably, IISc, founded by Jamshedji Tata in 1911, always maintained Tata representatives on its council. Bhabha's lineage held a connection to the institution, as both his grandfather and father had served on the council.

However, tensions within the scientific community began to emerge. CV Raman, seeking funding from the Tata Trusts for nuclear physics research, faced refusal, as the trust had already allocated funds to Meghnad Saha for similar research in Calcutta.

This disagreement between Saha and Raman set the stage for future discord that would affect various aspects of scientific research in India.

The seeds of a potential rift between Saha and Bhabha were possibly sown earlier, likely during the late 1930s. Saha, known for his pioneering work on the ionisation of gas in the 1920s, was a prominent figure in astrophysics. In 1938, he joined the IISc Council. Saha invited Bhabha to Calcutta University in April 1940, expressing a strong desire to discuss cosmic rays and work closely on related matters. Bhabha accepted this invitation, leading to a series of lectures in Calcutta in December 1940.

Saha's amiable tone in his correspondence, welcoming Bhabha and even suggesting a possible joint vacation in Darjeeling for both discussion and cosmic ray research, laid the foundation for their interaction. This collaboration marked the beginning of an association between the two influential figures in the field of physics, despite the underlying tensions and differences that would emerge in the later years.

Saha's influence played a pivotal role in triggering the interest of both Allahabad and Calcutta universities, leading them to offer Bhabha a readership position. However, while considering these opportunities, Bhabha was deterred by the scorching heat prevalent during the summer months in these regions. He envisioned that these positions wouldn't provide him with the ample space necessary to build a distinguished and exceptional school of physics, an ambition close to his heart as outlined in his sentiments within 'Building Scientific Institutions in India: Saha and Bhabha.'

Meanwhile, Bhabha found a mentor in Raman, who immediately took a liking to him and extended support in establishing the cosmic ray research unit. This unit found its initial home in a veranda adjacent to the library at the institute. Bhabha led a committed team comprising enthusiastic students and workers dedicated to this venture.

Ever the seeker of diverse experiences, Bhabha's artistic curiosity led him to explore Bangalore's historical gems, specifically the ancient artwork adorning the temples of Belur and Halebid. His interest in India's art and architectural history was no fleeting fancy. He had previously ventured to various ancient sites like Elephanta, Ajanta caves, Ellora, Sanchi, and Fatehpur Sikri, meticulously sketching his observations. His appreciation for these historical sites and their architectural brilliance was a fundamental part of his character.

Renowned German cartoonist Rudolf von Leyden, who had moved to Bombay, recalled Bhabha's deep-rooted admiration for the beauty and historical significance of Delhi's landmarks. Bhabha often sought moments of respite at places like Hauz Khas, the Lodi Tombs, or in front of the splendid facade of Sher Shah's mosque at Purana Kila. His insight into architectural history was substantial, as highlighted by his explanation to British physicist Cecil Powell about the Belur-Halebid temples a decade later. Bhabha discussed how these temples embodied a late baroque style, distinct from the classical phase of Indian art, which he believed might have exhibited a more simplistic approach, sadly almost entirely lost in India compared to, for instance, ancient Egyptian remnants.

Moreover, Bhabha's fascination extended to modern architecture, a passion that significantly influenced the establishment of his own institute in Bombay. He expressed distress over the uninspired and tasteless office buildings that emerged in Indian cities post-independence. His conversations with von Leyden at Purana Quila reflected his dismay over the desecration of cityscapes by construction projects devoid of historical awareness or architectural elegance. Bhabha firmly believed that a partially ruined chhattri at the end of a crumbling wall held more historical significance than the post-independence buildings, all labelled with the suffix 'Bhavans.' This opinion underlined his deep reverence for historical architecture and his disdain for the architectural degradation he witnessed in modern constructions.

There is little documented evidence supporting Bhabha's inclination towards nationalist obligations at that time, despite often-cited official accounts. His primary aspiration lay in swiftly returning abroad, where he believed the true action resided. In a conversation with Millikan, he shared the news that his university was contemplating establishing a special chair specifically aimed at fostering research. The chair was designed to promote research endeavours in the university, providing substantial funds for experimental research—a prospect that genuinely intrigued Bhabha. He expressed his keenness to collaborate with Millikan and explore the possibilities at the California Institute of Technology, illustrating a strong desire to work there in an undated letter.

Furthermore, Bhabha anticipated visiting the United States eagerly and passionately wished for an opportunity to arise in the near future that would enable him to work at Millikan's institute. He communicated his predicament regarding financial constraints due to wartime restrictions in a letter to Millikan in March 1941. These restrictions hindered his ability to take adequate funds out of the country to cover expenses in the US. However, he remained optimistic about securing a passport, even though the ongoing war had complicated the process. Bhabha eagerly awaited the war's end, as it would pave the way for him to resume his scientific pursuits without impediment. Speculation regarding his departure for the US had even reached Cambridge.

By mid-1940, Bhabha had secured a grant from the Sir Dorabji Tata Trust to establish a unit for cosmic ray research. He corresponded with Polly about obtaining funds for high-altitude flights and expressed his desire to replicate some of Millikan's experiments. This marked a significant departure from his known work at Cambridge, where he stood out as a theoretical physicist among several distinguished experimentalists. The shift in focus was partly due to the unavailability of experimental data he had previously accessed at Cambridge. Initially, his work in Bangalore had a more mathematical orientation, which later transitioned to experimental pursuits in 1943.

The inspiration for this shift might be traced back to Millikan's visit to Bangalore between December 1939 and March 1940. Millikan, then almost 72 and a Nobel laureate in Physics in 1923 for his work on the charge of the electron, conducted cosmic ray experiments using the balloon technique in Bangalore, Agra, and Peshawar alongside his collaborators Victor Neher and William Henry Pickering from the California Institute of Technology. These experiments aimed to study the variation of primary cosmic rays near the geometric equator.

The India Meteorological Department (IMD) facilitated laboratory facilities for Millikan's experiments, conducted through balloon flights that were launched from Bangalore. Millikan's visit provided an invaluable opportunity for Bhabha and his colleagues to familiarise themselves with balloon techniques and conduct their experiments. This occasion catalysed Bhabha's engagement in cosmic ray theory in collaboration with the Mathematics department of Central College, especially with KS Iyenger, and BS Madhava Rao, who had a mathematical Tripos from Cambridge.

Taking advantage of the B29 aircraft available in Bangalore due to the Second World War, Bhabha ventured into experimental studies on cosmic rays. He delved into the latitude effects on mesons, exploring both the soft and hard components of cosmic rays. The soft component, encompassing electrons, positrons, and gamma rays, was well-described by cosmic ray shower theory. However, the hard component, primarily comprising mesons, demanded further experimental observations. Bhabha focused on the penetrating component's variation with altitude and constructed a 12-inch diameter cloud chamber to study the scattering properties of new mesons, collaborating with

MS Sinha. This marked a significant shift towards hands-on experimental work for Bhabha in the cosmic ray domain.

Music held a profound significance for Bhabha, offering him solace and strength in times of distress. His brother, Jamshed Bhabha, aptly likened Bhabha's connection to music to a deeply rooted religious devotion, portraying its role as a constant source of comfort and inspiration for him. During his tenure in Bangalore, Bhabha found solace in attending classical music concerts at Basavangudi, particularly the Sunday morning performances. His companion at these gatherings was Vikram Sarabhai, who would later emerge as a key figure in India's space programme. Despite a ten-year age gap, Sarabhai shared Bhabha's pursuit of physics, having also pursued studies at Cambridge. However, due to the disruptions caused by World War II, Sarabhai returned to India after completing his Tripos examination in 1940 and commenced his doctoral studies under Raman's guidance, focusing on cosmic rays.

The urge to explore cosmic rays was instigated, in part, by Robert Millikan's lectures in 1940 during his visit to India for cosmic ray data collection. Millikan, recognised for coining the term 'cosmic rays,' debated the nature of cosmic rays, positing them as high-energy gamma ray photons while others speculated they were primarily particles. The hypothesis was tested regarding the variation of cosmic ray flux with latitude. The collected data eventually confirmed that cosmic rays consisted mainly of charged particles, supporting the particle model.

Millikan's visit to Bangalore not only reinforced this understanding but also prompted Raman and Sarabhai to recognise the significance of southern India for cosmic ray investigations. The proximity of the magnetic equator in the southern tip of the Indian subcontinent made it an intriguing location for such studies. Sarabhai, in pursuit of this research, constructed a Geiger Counter and presented his initial paper at a 1941 Indian Academy of Sciences meeting.

Bhabha and Sarabhai shared commonalities beyond their cosmic ray research fervour. Originating from western India, both hailed from influential industrialist families and had studied at Cambridge, naturally fostering a strong affinity between them. Their camaraderie extended to evenings spent at the distinguished West End hotel, frequented by Bhabha during his subsequent visits to Bangalore. The duo often socialised with local friends, including Anil D'Silva, an attractive Sri Lankan lady. Reflecting on those times, Sivaraj Ramaseshan, Raman's nephew, reminisced about how the more conservative students, predominantly middle-class Tamil Brahmins, observed them with a mixture of admiration and envy. Bhabha's unorthodox work habits also stood out, as he laboured late into the night, arriving at the institute in the afternoon, a schedule that intrigued many.

During the tumultuous 17th century, a pivotal transformation took place in England amid civil strife and the catastrophic devastation of the Great Fire of London. This era bore witness to a revolution, not just in terms of political and societal upheaval, but also in the realm of science and knowledge. It marked the demise of an age dominated by superstition and mystical beliefs, making way for a new era centred on rational thinking, scientific experimentation, and empirical evidence.

At the forefront of this intellectual resurgence stood the Royal Society, often recognised as the pioneering beacon of modern Western science. Its roots trace back to a series of gatherings among natural philosophers in influential academic centres like Oxford and London. Among the luminaries participating in these gatherings were eminent figures such as Sir Christopher Wren and the illustrious Sir Isaac Newton.

These intellectual congregations culminated in the formal establishment of the Royal Society, which received a significant endorsement in the form of a royal charter from King Charles II. This royal imprimatur bestowed the Society with the distinguished title by which it is now renowned: The Royal Society. The favour and support extended by the monarchy persisted across successive reigns, ensuring the institution's esteemed status.

The Royal Society holds the distinguished honour of being the United Kingdom's preeminent National Academy of Sciences. As the oldest national scientific institution globally, its fellowship remains a mark of immense prestige. Election as a fellow to this venerable society has historically been and continues to be regarded as a notable recognition of exceptional contributions in the realm of scientific endeavours.

Raman's nomination and Dirac's seconding catapulted Bhabha into the esteemed ranks of the Royal Society in 1941, a remarkable achievement at the young age of 32. Raman, keenly aware of Bhabha's multifaceted nature, introduced him to the Indian scientific community at the Indian Academy of Sciences meeting in Nagpur. Describing Bhabha as a fervent music enthusiast, a talented artist, an exceptional engineer, and an outstanding scientist, Raman likened him to the modern-day counterpart of Leonardo da Vinci.

Despite his busy schedule, Bhabha ardently yearned to return to England. Following Millikan's departure, Bhabha expressed his longing for more favourable conditions conducive to scientific pursuits. He explored the possibility of visiting the United States, but due to wartime financial constraints, Millikan couldn't secure funding for such a trip. Bhabha expressed his isolation in India, emphasising his ambition to establish a school. However, the gravity of the ongoing war overshadowed the significance of pure research, prompting him to anticipate a return to England.

Initially, owing to the lack of accessible data in Bangalore, Bhabha concentrated on theoretical work, leveraging ideas from his time at Cambridge. Addressing a gap in Dirac's electron theory, which didn't account for spin, Bhabha endeavoured to extend Dirac's work. His focus lay in examining the impact of radiation's feedback on an accelerating particle, especially the complexities surrounding spinning electrons and the interplay between rigid-body dynamics and relativity.

Bhabha collaborated with H.C. Corben in Cambridge to explore this challenge, as suggested by Dirac himself. Their approach involved modifying the definition of energy for point particles, leading to their first joint paper titled 'General classical theory of spinning particles in a Maxwell field' in 1940. Subsequently, Bhabha expanded this work to address mesons, discovering that radiation's back-reaction decreased collision effectiveness at high energies. This finding contradicted assumptions derived from classical theory, revealing that collision rates tapered off at higher energy levels, contrasting the anticipated increase based on classical predictions.

Bhabha's journey into theoretical physics, his attempts to reconcile theoretical models with the observed experimental phenomena, and his early contributions to particle physics unveiled the depth of his scientific acumen and paved the way for his influential work in the realm of theoretical physics.

In August 1941, Bhabha was extended an offer to occupy the prestigious chair of physics at Allahabad University. However, he politely declined the offer, expressing a strong aversion to the routine responsibilities of daily teaching and the meticulous administrative duties associated with the position. There were several reasons contributing to his refusal. It's possible that Bhabha was disinclined due to his anticipated elevation to a full professorship in Bangalore, a distinction potentially tied to his recent election to the Royal Society.

Interestingly, the position in Allahabad was also proposed to Krishnan and S Chandrasekhar, both of whom turned down the offer. Even the renowned physicist Schrödinger was considered a viable candidate for the post, although he opted for an appointment as a professor of theoretical physics in Dublin. The Vice-Chancellor at Allahabad University seemed exceedingly optimistic about securing Schrödinger's services, to the extent that he prematurely announced the acquisition of the esteemed scientist, assuming that his eminence was universally acknowledged and certain to join the university faculty.

Bhabha's tenure at IISc witnessed the development of outstanding pupils, including the remarkable Subodh Kumar Chakrabarti, with whom he coincidentally was of age. Before becoming affiliated with Bhabha, Chakrabarti held a position as an instructor at the University of Calcutta. Saha, acknowledging his prowess, recommended that he work in Bangalore with Bhabha to further investigate the cascade theory of air showers.

The objective of their partnership was to bridge the distance between the empirical observations and the predictions formulated by Bhabha and Heitler in their previous collaboration by integrating new experimental data. Published in 1942 as part of a series of studies, their collaborative paper entitled "Calculations on cascade theory with collision loss," provided a critical evaluation of the inconsistencies that existed between theory and practise. They emphasised that the theoretical framework's imprecision was frequently attributable to errors stemming from physical assumptions and mathematical approximations, whereas the experimental data itself was fraught with uncertainty.

One of the primary obstacles encountered was the need to account for energy loss caused by collisions, which is often disregarded. Prior endeavours by researchers H. Snyder and R. Serber to integrate this phenomenon had resulted in a sequence of terms lacking a definitive method for deriving a sum. Chakrabarti and Bhabha attempted to resolve this issue by employing novel mathematical techniques and conducting a comprehensive assessment of the impact of energy loss within the framework of cascade theory. By bridging the distance between theory and experimental data, this methodical approach sought to improve calculations and further the understanding of air shower phenomena.

Homi Bhabha had resided in Bangalore for approximately five years by 1945, having progressed from being a reader to a full-time professor in 1944. As soon as the conflict ended, the international scientific community endeavoured to resume its scientific pursuits. The anticipation of Bhabha's return in England was palpable, as indicated by Maurice Pryce's support, which consisted of disseminating the news of the Wykeham Professorship in Oxford and compelling Bhabha to contemplate his application; Pryce emphasised the potential advantages that such a position could bring to English theoretical physics.

Concurrently, India's independence movement had amassed considerable momentum, indicating a forthcoming shift towards self-governance. As Bhabha reflected on his responsibilities beyond the laboratory's boundaries, he started to consider the structure and trajectory of scientific inquiry in an independent India. At this critical juncture, Bhabha underwent a realisation of a wider scope, transcending his present research on cosmic radiation.

Greenstein eloquently describes this aspect of Bhabha's life, arguing that his repatriation to India offered an optimal environment for him to cultivate his proclivity for establishing institutions and engage in extensive administration—opportunities that would not have been as readily available in England, with its well-established scientific establishments. In contrast, India offered a significant vacuum in this domain, which provided an opportunity for Bhabha's dormant administrative prowess to thrive. Furthermore, their arrival in India during a pivotal moment, when the impending independence of the nation was tangible, sparked an environment brimming with limitless potential and shared fervour.

Bhabha was not the only visionary who pondered the prospective trajectory of scientific inquiry in India. During his time in Bangalore, notable individuals including Meghnad Saha and Shanti Swarup Bhatnagar were similarly deliberating on the critical necessity for a focused scientific endeavour, particularly with India's impending independence in mind. The convergence of these ideas and their shared aspirations inspired Bhabha to investigate more expansive schemes and their broader ramifications for scientific advancement in India.

In the 1930s, there was a strong desire among scientists, like Raman, to establish research institutions in India. However, the British government was dismissive, deeming such steps as unnecessary. Instead, an Industrial Intelligence and Research Bureau was established for testing and instrument quality. Bhatnagar, its first director, had a vision of aligning scientific research with industrial needs, but even this bureau was slated for closure at the war's onset. It took the persistent efforts of Arcot Ramaswamy Mudaliar to advocate for the formation of the Council of Scientific and Industrial Research (CSIR) in 1942, which led to Bhatnagar's suggestion for establishing national laboratories.

During this time, Saha, too, was contemplating broader prospects for scientific research in India, extending beyond his laboratory work. He was instrumental in shaping the distinction between scientific and industrial research. This was paralleled by the formation of the National Planning Committee (NPC) with Jawaharlal Nehru as chair, focusing on issues like industrial self-sufficiency, yet it faltered due to wartime upheaval.

Notably, in 1944, a group of industrialists published the 'Bombay Plan,' proposing a mixed economy. In the midst of these developments, Bhabha envisioned a different approach. He sought to build an indigenous scientific research institution in India and expressed this desire to JRD Tata, urging that research institutions comparable to global standards were imperative.

Encouraged by JRD Tata's response, Bhabha, in a detailed letter to Sir Sorab Saklatvala, chairman of the Tata Trusts, advocated for a centralised school of research in fundamental physics. His vision encompassed gathering competent researchers under proper direction to enhance the quality of applied research in India, fostering excellence and advisory roles in research endeavours.

This proposed institute would not only advance theoretical and experimental physics but also drive practical applications in industry, marking a significant stride in uplifting India's research landscape.

Bhabha took a leap in seeking philanthropic funding from patrons like the Tatas, although it wasn't without some hesitance on his part. In a candid admission to JRD Tata, he confessed abandoning modesty to advocate for a science-backed initiative he believed in, acknowledging it as a bold step.

JRD Tata's response was reassuring, lightening the tone and implying that their business circles were not startled by such forms of self-promotion. He subtly underplayed Bhabha's apprehension, remarking it was almost inaudible, hinting at their readiness to support such proposals.

When invited to join a scientific delegation to the UK, the USA, and Canada, Bhabha declined, realising the pressing need for planning his institute. He was well-acquainted with international scientific practices but was singularly dedicated to reshaping the research environment in India.

During his discussion with Sir AV Hill, suggestions to include biophysics were made, recognising India's biological needs, yet Bhabha's focus at that moment remained primarily on physics. His aspirations for nuclear power production were evident, envisioning India nurturing its own experts once nuclear energy applications took root.

Eventually, the Tata Trusts agreed to establish a fundamental research institute in 1945, contingent upon contributions from Bombay University and the government. JRD Tata advocated for Bhabha's cause during the Trusts meeting, a strategic move to create an alliance between the government, the university system, and private enterprise in alignment with the Bombay Plan's objectives.

The formal establishment of the Tata Institute of Fundamental Research took place on 1 June, initially in Bangalore before relocating to south Bombay within six months. The institute settled at Kenilworth, a residence on Peddar Road, owned by Bhabha's aunt, Cooverbai Panday. Half of the house was rented for Rs 200 per month to accommodate the institute. It's interesting to note that this very house was where Bhabha himself was born, and coincidentally, the room of his birth became his office within the institute's premises. The institute was inaugurated on 19 December 1945, with the event being graced by Sir John Colville, the Governor of Bombay at the time.

In his inaugural address, Bhabha revisited his foundational thoughts that were shaped during his student years, influenced particularly by Bernal's concept of the social function of science. He emphasised the vital role of science in modern society, stating that it's no longer an auxiliary discipline but forms the bedrock of our entire social structure. Drawing from Marx's words on humanity's power over nature shaping history, Bhabha highlighted how scientific advancements have steered the course of the world. He stressed the importance of scientific progress, not only in empirical terms but also in expanding our philosophical understanding and challenging conventional, sense-based ideas. Bhabha emphasised that the study of cosmic radiation was the primary field of experimental research at the institute, envisioning the extension of this work into nuclear physics shortly.

Bhabha expressed the critical role of philosophy, logic, and mathematics in comprehensively representing human experiences, underlining their power in forming the future's mental discipline. He pointed out the significance of theoretical work and the creation of new mathematics, envisaging that these would form a more crucial part of future education compared to outdated languages or archaic forms of logic.

Tata Institute of Fundamental Research

The Tata Institute of Fundamental Research (TIFR) began its operations in the cosmic ray unit of the Indian Institute of Science (IISc), which was a temporary arrangement. The plan was to establish the institution in Bombay, but finding suitable premises proved challenging. Through connections, Bhabha's aunt, Cooverbai Panday, offered to rent half of her 6,000 square feet bungalow for a monthly rent of ₹500, facilitating the institute's initial home in Bombay.

This relocation had a personal touch as the room housing Bhabha's office in the bungalow was the very room where he was born. The temporary nature of starting the work first and then establishing a permanent building was evident in these initial arrangements. The bungalow, which housed TIFR, later made way for an apartment complex known as Kenilworth, developed in 1962-63. The Directorate of Estates (DE) finished constructing

Kenilworth in 1962-63 and the Department of Atomic Energy (DAE) allocated flats on April 1, 1964.

An intriguing story persists that after TIFR shifted to Kenilworth, the building was sold. The new owner supposedly transformed it into a hotel with the same name. When put up for sale again, Bhabha acquired the building for the AEC, constructing flats for staff. The building's peculiar shape, the layout of the flats, and other distinct features reinforce the credibility of this story.

To transition to the new location in 1945, TIFR's provisional council, during its second meeting, arranged for Bhabha's equipment to be shipped from Bangalore to Bombay. Bhabha negotiated with JC Ghosh, the director of IISc, and the Trust offered a grant of ₹50,000 to IISc in exchange for the old cosmic ray equipment and personnel to manage it, along with additional instruments. The laboratory assistant and the glass blower also moved to Bombay with the new setup. When discussing the move to Bombay, Bhabha personally asked the laboratory assistant to relocate. The assistant initially sought his father's permission, to which his father responded, "When Bhabha is asking, why can't you say yes? Why ask me?" - indicating the significance and authority of Bhabha's request.

The institute was inaugurated on December 19, 1945, with distinguished guests such as JRD and Naval Tata, Jahangir D. Choksi, and several other notable figures in attendance. Saklatvala, welcoming the governor to the provisional establishment, acknowledged the lingering shadow of war that hung over the world. He stressed that despite lacking a permanent building, the institute had already commenced experimental and theoretical physics work.

It was underscored that a scientific institution's distinction, at that time, was more about its reputation in the eyes of the public, based on the intellectual achievements of its personnel. The Trust displayed immense confidence in Bhabha's capabilities, recognising the importance of both scientific achievements and the individual behind the institute.

During the inaugural ceremony, Bhabha delivered a speech that, though free of technical jargon, was abstract and complex, not intended for the layperson. He outlined the trajectory of physics, the six elementary particles known then (electron, proton, neutron, Meson, neutrino, and photon), and the substantial progress in mathematical descriptions of known elemental particles. Bhabha highlighted the importance of theories predicting new phenomena and guiding experimental discoveries, citing James Maxwell's equations for photons in the 19th century and Dirac's equations for electrons in 1928 as significant examples.

In his inaugural address, Bhabha revisited his earlier thoughts influenced by Bernal's concept of the social role of science. He emphasised that science, along with its practical applications, had taken on a paramount role in society. Bhabha echoed Marx's statement that "man's power over nature is at the root of history," illustrating that countries with significant scientific advancement have moulded global history. He underlined that scientific progress not only holds practical importance but also a philosophical significance by expanding our mental horizons and challenging conventional, sensory-based understanding.

Highlighting cosmic radiation as the primary focus of experimental research at the institute, Bhabha anticipated a future expansion into nuclear physics. He emphasised the significance of mathematical formalism in conveying complex thoughts that evade verbal expression. Bhabha outlined the importance of theoretical work, incorporating the creation and application of new mathematics in the comprehension of the natural world. He firmly believed that these precise theories, encapsulating concentrated knowledge, would serve as the foundation for the mental education of future generations, eclipsing the study of obsolete languages or outdated forms of logic.

Bhabha, even while awaiting a response from the Tatas, had already started considering the specifics. He reached out to renowned astrophysicist Subrahmanyan Chandrasekhar, inviting him to join the institute upon its establishment. Although Chandrasekhar politely declined the offer, Bhabha was proactively forming plans.

In 1945, a group of scientists established the Atomic Energy Committee, sponsored by CSIR, to investigate India's atomic energy resources and advise on their utilisation. Bhabha was appointed as its chairman, with other notable scientists like Bhatnagar, Saha, Krishnan, and Satyendra Nath Bose as members. These deliberations occurred before the USA's atomic bomb test and the bombings in Japan. The committee was keen on creating three nuclear research institutes: one in Delhi, another in Calcutta supervised by Saha (where a cyclotron was under construction), and one in Bombay, to be established at Bhabha's institute. By 1946, the committee began its meetings in Bombay.

The institute's funding followed the 'Bhabha formula,' employing a triangular finance-sharing method among the Tata Trusts, the local government (later the government of Maharashtra), and the government of India. This approach was recommended by the Tata Trusts and was previously employed at the Indian Institute of Science, where finances were contributed by the Tata Trusts, the government of Mysore, and the government of India. The initial budget for TIFR's first year (1945-46) was Rs 80,000, with Rs 45,000 from the Tata Trusts, Rs 25,000 from the government of Bombay, and Rs 10,000 from CSIR.

Upon establishing the new institute, Bhabha meticulously continued the research programme initiated in Bangalore, ensuring the transfer of cosmic ray research equipment to Bombay. To aid in this endeavour, he secured local assistance from the University of Bombay. Collaborations were initiated, notably with Professor Taylor from Wilson College, who shared a keen interest in cosmic rays. Bhabha also benefitted from the support of Father Raphael at St. Xavier's College, who offered two of his associates to aid in assembling the components of the cloud chamber obtained from Bangalore. Among his talented recruits was HLN Murthy from IISc, initially employed as a glassblower but later recognised by Bhabha for his adept instrument fabrication skills. Recognising Murthy's expertise, Bhabha even arranged for his advanced training at Bristol in England.

Moreover, Bhabha's strategic plans encompassed the construction of an accelerator for particle experiments. The objective was to examine particles at high-energy levels by accelerating them and observing their collisions for indications of their properties. However, achieving high-energy levels was a complex feat, requiring substantial instruments where particles could be manipulated using strong magnetic fields. While a cyclotron was in progress in Calcutta, persistent issues hindered its completion. Bhabha considered procuring a Betatron machine from General Electric, similar to Enrico Fermi's attempts in Chicago. CSIR offered financial support of Rs 40,000 for this purpose in 1946. Yet, Bhabha's hopes were dashed due to a sudden US government embargo on the export of accelerators, a setback also faced by Fermi.

Subsequently, with the setback in acquiring a Betatron, Bhabha revisited his earlier concept of airborne instruments to study cosmic rays. However, the Indian air force planes were unavailable for his use. This compelled Bhabha to explore utilising balloons to elevate his instruments for this purpose. Given India's proximity to the magnetic equator, the Earth's magnetic field diverted low-energy particles, enabling the detection of high-energy particles with precision through instruments carried aloft by balloons. Additionally, India's mountainous terrain provided an optimal setting for high-altitude cosmic ray research, allowing extended studies in balloon flights and at mountaintop stations.

Notably, India's abundant mines were also utilised for cosmic ray studies. Placing instruments at the base of these mines facilitated the filtration of particles absorbed by the upper crust, enabling the detection of particles not impeded by such absorption. Bhabha assembled a team specifically for this project, engaging individuals already employed for other purposes to contribute to balloon experiments.

Bhabha recognised the suitability of this research path within the Indian context due to its requirement for relatively moderate financial resources, facilitating cutting-edge research. Moreover, such initiatives would provide India with the opportunity to acquire modern experimental physics methodologies. Additionally, these activities aimed to instil confidence among young Indian scientists, demonstrating that they could attain scientific accomplishments despite challenges like financial constraints, limited technical experience, or the absence of a robust tradition in experimental sciences.

Bhabha continued his work on theoretical projects, publishing his initial paper from the new institute, introducing the Bhabha equation in a special edition of Reviews of Modern Physics in 1945, marking Niels Bohr's 60th birthday. Collaborating with Chakrabarti, he expanded his studies on cosmic ray showers.

At the behest of his former tutor Dirac, Bhabha recognised the necessity of a robust mathematics group to establish a theoretical physics programme within the institute. Actively seeking talented young mathematicians to join his venture, Bhabha established a formidable mathematics department at TIFR, which remains among the nation's best to this day. The early members of this department included Damodar D. Kosambi, whose interdisciplinary interests spanned mathematics, history, and archaeology, significantly impacting Indian historical studies. Additionally, K. Chandrasekharan, affiliated with the prestigious Institute of Advanced Studies in Princeton, and Pesi Masani, were notable mathematicians who joined Bhabha's initiative.

However, the period in India was fraught with turmoil due to the impending partition, threatening communal harmony and resulting in riots in Bombay. In a letter to Bhabha, who was overseas in late 1946, Kosambi provided an update: "Bombay has yet to recover from three months of rioting and looting of shops. I observed significant unrest in severely affected areas at least twice a week. As a result, there is no concrete accomplishment to show, although Thatte's cosmic ray counters are almost ready for completion."

In India, Bhabha actively sought promising young science students by spreading the word through various channels. As noted by science historian Robert Anderson, the encounters with Bhabha were varied, occurring at colleges, universities, or even railway station platforms, wherever a meeting seemed feasible. Potential candidates found themselves both hesitant and intimidated before their interviews, yet they were surprised by Bhabha's attentive listening and willingness to engage. Invited candidates found themselves integrated into Bhabha's expanding network and eventually became his colleagues. Notably, Bhabha didn't consider any of them as 'his students' in the traditional sense; he aimed to bridge the class and rank gap between him and these budding scientists. Setting up a unique "school," he offered rigorous retraining sessions, alternating between Bombay and Bangalore to foster specialised talent.

Among these individuals was B.V. Sreekantan, a student from IISc, Bangalore, who later became the director of TIFR. During Sreekantan's interview with Bhabha, he was torn between pursuing theoretical or experimental physics and left the decision to Bhabha. Acknowledging Sreekantan's expertise in electronics, Bhabha suggested a path toward experimental physics, respecting Sreekantan's ultimate choice. Inspired by Bhabha's guidance, Sreekantan made the decision to join TIFR despite its lacking infrastructure.

With Sreekantan's assistance, Bhabha established a cosmic ray experimental facility within the Kolar Gold Mines, located at a depth of 3 kilometres, making it one of the deepest mines globally. This endeavour aimed to explore the changes in cosmic ray intensity with varying depths beneath the Earth's surface, focusing on the prevalence of muons, the most abundant particles detected on the Earth's surface. This initiative marked India's first deep underground laboratory, although later it was discovered that the muons detected did not originate from cosmic rays but rather from the Earth's atmosphere, challenging the initial hypothesis.

Moreover, the institute attracted students from diverse universities, welcoming a steady influx of talent from other institutions. Many visitors eventually transitioned to become faculty members, such as A.S. Rao from Benaras Hindu University, D.Y. Phadake from a technical institute in Bombay, and Dharmatti from RIS, Bombay.

When India gained its independence, the event was marked with a simple flag hoisting ceremony at Kennilworth. Vasudev, a chairholder, mentioned that Bhabha had given him a flag the night before the Independence Day to raise on the terrace of the institute. However, when Bhabha arrived and inquired about the flag, he discovered it had already been unfurled. Bhabha remarked that on the first day of independence, it's not about unfurling the flag but rather raising it. Consequently, they raised the flag and sang the national anthem. Independence brought about a shift in the relationship between scientists and the state. Bhabha expected his scientists to embrace a broader form of nationalism, aligning themselves with the universe of science that transcended national boundaries.

In early January 1948, the mathematician F.W. Levi joined Kosambi at TIFR. A Jewish refugee from the Nazi regime, Levi was an expert in algebra, particularly the theory of groups. His teaching background from 1920 to 1935 ended when the Nazi government dismissed him due to his Jewish heritage. In 1935, he took up an offer as the head of the mathematics department at the University of Calcutta. According to mathematician Raghavan Narasimhan, Levi had a significant impact on the development of 20th-century mathematics in India, notably by introducing modern algebra at Calcutta University.

Bhabha was pleased to welcome Levi at TIFR, allowing the institution to facilitate research on modern algebra and function theory. In August 1947, Levi delivered lectures at TIFR, and his arrival in 1948 aligned with Bhabha's plan for mathematics at the institute. Although Bhabha had invited Dirac's student Christie Jayaratnam Eliezer to TIFR, Eliezer, then teaching in Cambridge, declined due to commitments in Ceylon. Notable progress in mathematics was later achieved when mathematician K. Chandrasekharan joined TIFR in 1949, a development that will be discussed in a subsequent chapter.

❑

The Atomic Revolution

The narrative of the nuclear programme initiated with the establishment of the Atomic Energy Committee in 1946, which included members such as Bhatnagar, Saha, Darashaw Nosherwan Wadia, DM Bose, Nazir Ahmad, and KS Krishnan. Bhabha had been a proponent of such a committee, and it's probable that his influence on Sir Ardeshir Dalal, the president of the CSIR governing body, led to its creation under the CSIR's aegis. Initially named the Atomic Energy Committee, its designation was later altered to the Atomic Energy Research Committee, considering nuclear physics as a novel field in India with limited expertise. A Board of Research on Atomic Energy was also established, having Bhabha and Saha as its members. The committee convened in Bombay and was sustained by funding from the CSIR on behalf of the committee's operations.

During the pre-independence period, an Atomic Energy Committee was already in place, operating under the umbrella of CSIR, with Bhabha serving as its chair. It was in 1946, in the wake of the atomic bombings in Japan, that discussions about India's nuclear resources and their utilisation commenced in Bombay. Various nations, following these atomic events, began actively developing nuclear technologies, and secrecy enveloped these pursuits, with each country guarding their interests, particularly for military applications of nuclear power.

The scientists in India saw this global atmosphere as a promising opportunity. They recognised that the UK was not within the purview of American nuclear plans and observed the UK and the Soviet Union making strides in establishing their nuclear reactors. Each of these countries had already established atomic energy commissions. The British government in India did not overtly object to or interfere with the activities of Indian scientists concerning nuclear power, possibly more concerned about the imminent independence or underestimating the scientists' potential. Despite their apparent lack of intervention, they were mindful of the scientific advancements happening in India.

A pivotal moment in the post-World War II era was the sequence of goodwill missions involving Indian scientists and industrialists, fostering global scientific exchanges with the UK, the US, and Canada. Among these missions, a notable scientific expedition in 1945 brought together seven eminent scientists and industry administrators, including Ahmad, Bhatnagar, JC Ghosh, and Saha. Notably absent was Raman, sparking criticism due to his non-participation.

The initial phase of this mission involved a comprehensive two-month visit to various scientific and industrial facilities in the UK before progressing to the subsequent part of their itinerary in the US. The US leg included tours to various laboratories, including the Ernest Lawrence Radiation Laboratory, where the classified atomic bomb research was underway, prompting stringent secrecy measures. Despite the constraints, Saha, who remained vigilant, noted the vague awareness and close proximity to some atomic sites during their visit. This curiosity led to suspicion, resulting in Saha being questioned by the FBI about his knowledge of nuclear fission and its potential wartime application. The mission also included visits to the USSR in June 1945, coinciding with the 220th anniversary of the Russian Academy of Sciences, inspiring hope for post-war reconstruction and influencing discussions on state-led scientific initiatives in India.

Subsequently, the second goodwill mission took the form of participation in the Empire Scientific Conference, immediately following the inaugural meeting of the Atomic Energy Research Committee (AERC) in May 1946. Bhabha's presence at this conference was significant, considering the global scientific synergy fostered during the Second World War. This conference aimed to sustain the productive collaboration among scientists from the British Empire, involving three weeks under the Royal Society's leadership and two weeks managed by the British Commonwealth official scientific conference. Attended by a global delegation, this conference, inaugurated by George VI, spanned a week in London, Oxford, and Cambridge, focusing on encouraging free and transparent scientific exchanges without bureaucratic or nationalistic barriers. Leading the Indian delegation was Bhatnagar, as Raman abstained, expressing his reservations about acknowledging national institutions as representatives of Indian science. Bhabha delved into discussions on cosmic ray research, while Saha contributed insights on disseminating scientific information within the empire.

During these series of meetings and events, an underlying tension simmered between Saha and Bhabha, further exacerbated by disagreements surrounding the AERC's subsequent decisions, signifying the divergence of their viewpoints and approaches.

In early 1947, Patrick Blackett met with Bhabha and Nehru, briefing the viceroy about the "atomic energy setup in India."

The period post-Independence in India witnessed significant advancements in nuclear research and resource discovery. In February 1947, geologist DN Wadia informed the committee about the extensive thorium reserves found in Kerala's monazite-rich beaches. Although uranium was not abundant in India, the vast thorium reserves presented a strategic advantage. However, thorium alone couldn't power a nuclear reactor due to its physical properties; it needed conversion to uranium (233) in a reactor before being utilised as fuel.

Bhabha took steps to experiment with nuclear fuel by requesting a tonne of crude uranium oxide from the National Research Council of Canada in June 1947. This effort involved a complex understanding between the USA, UK, and Canada, leading to the shipment of uranium to India. The arrangement perhaps aimed to potentially gain access to India's thorium supply in the future. Bhabha's connections, particularly with W.B. Lewis, head of Atomic Energy of Canada Limited and an old friend from Cambridge, were influential in facilitating this uranium shipment.

Immediately after India's independence, the Board of Research on Atomic Energy was established on August 26, 1947, with Bhabha as its chairman. Subsequently, in April 1948, Nehru introduced legislation in the Constituent Assembly, formulated in collaboration with Bhabha and Bhatnagar. This laid the groundwork for the establishment of the AEC in India, modelled closely after British and American atomic energy bills.

Nehru emphasised the necessity of secrecy around nuclear research and the government's absolute monopoly on such research. There was an underlying understanding that there was a connection between peaceful nuclear applications and potential military uses. In response to the debate in the Constituent Assembly, Nehru acknowledged the military component in India's nuclear programme from its inception but also emphasised India's need to collaborate with more advanced countries in nuclear physics, which required maintaining certain aspects in secrecy.

There was a visible conflict between Meghnad Saha and the trio of Nehru, Bhabha, and Bhatnagar regarding the focus and structure of India's nuclear research programme. Saha, due to his outspoken nature, gradually found himself at odds with the powers that influenced the direction of India's nuclear research. He criticised the idea of concentrating nuclear research in a single institution and opposed the choice of Bombay as the centre for nuclear research in India, citing its coastal location as potentially dangerous. He perceived this concentration as a dangerous move influenced by Bhabha and Bhatnagar, which could potentially make nuclear research irrelevant.

Saha believed that nuclear research should be conducted across several universities and institutes, similar to the approach taken in other countries, like the UK, where several universities were selected for atomic energy research under the supervision of various scientists. In contrast, Bhabha's model was a top-down, centralised approach concentrated in one institute in Bombay, a structure Saha believed would lead to disconnected ivory towers rather than integrated, practically applied research.

Saha's perspective emphasised growing nuclear physics capability from the ground up, advocating for the teaching of nuclear physics in universities and training talented students, a model he felt would better serve India's need for independent industrial strength. However, Saha's opinions did not gain much traction at the time. The policymakers either found his arguments unconvincing or considered him a dissenting voice and subsequently sidelined his suggestions.

In hindsight, some of Saha's concerns proved valid. The decision to centralise nuclear research in one location and separate research institutions from educational centres did raise challenges, and some consequences aligned with Saha's predictions. Yet, at that time, he was perceived as a lone dissenter and was marginalised from the decision-making process.

The tension between Saha and Bhabha had other underlying facets, notably regarding Saha's son, Ajitkumar, who was studying nuclear physics and was considered by Saha to be one of India's potential future nuclear scientists. Saha shared updates on his son's thesis progress with Bhabha, who in response insinuated a potential case of nepotism. He emphasised the importance of experimental nuclear physics over theoretical work, suggesting that their strengths lay in theoretical planning rather than in judging experimental techniques or their practical execution.

In his retort, Saha refuted the notion that he was primarily a theorist, highlighting his hands-on experience in performing various experiments in spectroscopy and thermal ionisation. The perception that Saha was more of a theorist could have stemmed from a notion inherited from Raman's time, as Raman had made similar comments. This might have been one of the tactics employed by Bhabha to diminish Saha's role in the field of nuclear physics and establish his own prominence.

Bhabha had cultivated a close relationship with Jawaharlal Nehru over the years, and their bond deepened gradually. Although the exact timing of their initial meeting is unclear, it's possible they interacted earlier, potentially at the house of Sir Dorabji Tata, where industrialists met nationalist leaders for discussions. Over time, their rapport became close, as evidenced by their informal addresses to each other as 'Dear Bhai' and 'Dear Homi'. Indira Gandhi recollected in a speech that Bhabha played a significant role in her father's life, providing a relaxed and different perspective amid the demands of political life.

Bhabha's influence was notable in his ability to convey the urgency of nuclear research to Nehru. Nehru, in turn, chose to engage exclusively with Bhabha by listening to his thoughts on 'The organisation of atomic research in India' after his return from an international visit. This interaction highlighted Bhabha's persuasive ability to influence and gain the attention of key figures like Nehru in matters related to nuclear research.

Homi Bhabha not only aimed to centralise nuclear research under his leadership but also sought the AEC to operate independently, free from the jurisdiction of the CSIR, which was under Shanti Swaroop Bhatnagar's control. Bhabha, eager to have a free hand in nuclear research, was assisted by Nehru, who paved the way by introducing the Atomic Energy Bill. Although a few more years passed before the formal establishment of a separate Department of Atomic Energy in August 1954, this bill laid the groundwork for Bhabha's significant authority in nuclear research in India.

The Atomic Energy Commission was officially constituted with the passing of the Atomic Energy Act in August 1948. The commission aimed to explore nuclear resources, harness them for industrial applications, create a nuclear reactor within five years, and foster the development of nuclear technology in laboratories. Nehru initially attempted to include Meghnad Saha in the commission, but Saha declined, opting to persist with teaching and training nuclear physicists as he had done previously.

Bhabha's recommendation led to the AEC's autonomy, being separate from any other government ministry or department and having its own secretariat. The commission, comprising three members - Bhabha as chairman, Bhatnagar as secretary, and KS Krishnan as an additional member, operated without involvement from bureaucrats. An allocation of one crore rupees was provided for the next three to five years, enabling Bhabha to vigorously pursue his nuclear research programme under this new institutional framework.

Homi Bhabha envisioned a comprehensive plan to leverage India's abundant thorium reserves in nuclear reactors. Nuclear reactors necessitate a fissile material, an element whose atomic nucleus becomes susceptible to splitting upon interaction with a neutron. While uranium (specifically U-235, with the adjacent number signifying the total particles in the nucleus) is a fissile material, naturally occurring uranium mostly consists of U-238, with three additional neutrons in its nucleus. Only a small fraction, about 0.7 percent, is U-235 in natural uranium. U-238 can become fissile through fast neutrons; however, in reactors with moderators that slow down neutrons, U-238 remains unaffected, while only U-235 undergoes fission.

In nuclear reactor operation, some U-238 gets converted into Plutonium-239, a man-made element that is not naturally available. This by-product is also fissile. By extracting this from used uranium reactor fuel, it can be used in a subsequent reactor. In the next-generation reactor, Pu-239 is combined with U-238. As power is generated, more fuel is transformed into Pu-239. This process allows the increase of Pu-239 reserves. These reactors, known as plutonium breeders, represent the second stage in Bhabha's plan.

Bhabha's vision included the development of Fast Breeder Reactors in the second stage. The idea is to sustain nuclear power production even after the depletion of uranium reserves globally, which is anticipated in a couple of centuries. The second stage would rely on burning plutonium, extending the life of nuclear power production through this strategic approach.

Homi Bhabha formulated a comprehensive plan to exploit India's vast thorium reserves for the future of nuclear power. His vision spanned three distinct stages in nuclear power generation, hinging on thorium's conversion into U-233, a fissile material. The first two stages focus on breeding materials necessary for energy production.

Stage 1 involved using uranium as a fuel. The subsequent creation of plutonium from the reactors in this stage is intended for the second stage, producing electricity and transforming thorium into U-233 or turning depleted uranium into additional plutonium, utilising breeding gains. The second-generation power stations aim to produce more U-233 than consumed during electricity production. The third-generation, breeder power stations are designed to generate more U-233 than utilised while generating power.

Although Bhabha's plan was primarily theoretical and there were no thorium-based reactors globally, he aimed to implement the plan step-by-step. The initial phase was exploring India's resources. The Atomic Energy Commission and the Geological Survey of India commenced exploration activities to discover nuclear fuel material. Furthermore, Indian Rare Earths Limited, a public-sector unit, was established in 1950 to process monazite minerals in Alwaye, Kerala. Significant uranium deposits were found in Jaduguda, Jharkhand, in 1951. Presently, India operates two uranium mines—Jaduguda and Tummalapalle in Andhra Pradesh.

For heavy water and related technology, Bhabha looked towards the United States and Canada. His acquaintance with W.B. Lewis from Cambridge was beneficial. Canada's research, initiated by Lewis, led to the creation of a heavy water moderated research reactor named NRX in Chalk River, Ontario, in 1947. This facility used natural uranium. Bhabha recognised the need for a reactor like NRX in India.

Bhabha's pursuit of collaboration led to discussions with France. Frédéric and Irène Joliot-Curie proposed a collaboration in 1950. France offered technical knowledge on uranium purification in exchange for India's export of thorium, beryllium, and mineral oil for graphite manufacture. This agreement was seen as a ground-breaking move, especially given the global secrecy surrounding nuclear technology. However, the British government and the United States were wary of the Indian-French collaboration and intended to sway India away from French influence.

This episode portrays the challenges and diplomatic complexities Bhabha faced in advancing India's nuclear agenda.

His diplomatic skills and network played a pivotal role in establishing collaborative efforts. His extensive connections and global exposure helped India navigate the intricate global politics surrounding atomic energy.

Homi Bhabha struck a significant deal with the UK that facilitated the construction of the APSARA swimming pool reactor. In 1955, the UK agreed to supply enriched uranium to India, laying the groundwork for substantial advancements in India's nuclear capabilities. An Indian team of scientists participated in the first International Course in Reactor Science and Technology in the UK. Furthermore, in the same year, Bhabha orchestrated the dispatch of a group comprising forty scientists and engineers to Canada for a year-long training in reactor technology.

The chosen site for these nuclear initiatives was the tranquil fishing village of Turbhe, known in its anglicised version as Trombay. This picturesque area was relatively isolated, bordered by hills that loomed as the tallest in Bombay, enhancing its security and seclusion. The selection of this crescent-shaped area was influenced by both security considerations and its serene aesthetic. Commencing in 1953, a thorium plant was established here, and construction of a swimming pool-type reactor utilising enriched uranium supplied by the UK began.

The AEC allocated funds for nuclear technology research, with some activities housed at the Kenilworth building of the Tata Institute of Fundamental Research (TIFR). Progressively, from around 1957, the focus shifted to the Trombay site, with most technological advancements being made there.

In recognition of his significant contributions, Bhabha was honoured with the Padmabhushan award by the Indian government in January 1954. This year also marked the establishment of the DAE, a move that Bhabha had been advocating for. Bhabha was appointed as the department's first secretary, placing it under the direct control of the Prime Minister. The DAE office was situated in Bombay, with a liaison office in New Delhi, marking a distinct deviation from the traditional norm of government offices being centralised in New Delhi. This bold move by Bhabha, locating the office outside New Delhi, was seen as unconventional by the bureaucratic standards prevailing in other government departments.

For Bhabha, the choice of having the DAE office in Bombay was logical. It allowed him to effectively oversee and orchestrate scientific research while keeping a considerable distance from the bureaucratic environment in New Delhi, which he disdained, identifying himself as a man of action rather than bureaucratic procedure. This innovative placement was a pioneering move that would later inspire a similar decision in the Department of Space (DoS), which established its headquarters in Bangalore rather than New Delhi.

As the United States had notably advanced in nuclear technology, emerging global players in this field were undeniable. After the Soviet Union conducted their atomic bomb test in 1949, followed by the UK in 1952, the Soviets further proceeded with a hydrogen bomb test in 1953. President Eisenhower, responding to these global developments, announced a strategic "Atoms for Peace" policy in December 1953 during his speech at the United Nations General Assembly. The primary objective of this policy was to extend assistance to other nations in the form of new technology for power generation and peaceful applications while cautiously ensuring that these technological advancements were not diverted toward the creation of nuclear weapons. This policy aimed to overturn the alarming secrecy and pervasive fear of nuclear warfare that prevailed in the post-World War II era.

The "Atoms for Peace" programme sought to reshape American policy by facilitating a transition to more open and cooperative approaches. Nonetheless, the implementation of this programme necessitated that participating nations adhered to certain controls and restrictions. Consequently, the USA proposed a resolution at the UN General Assembly, which received unanimous adoption in December 1954. The resolution initiated the proposal to establish an international atomic energy agency. Furthermore, it led to the formation of a Scientific Advisory Committee (SAC), comprising representatives from seven countries: the USA, the USSR, the UK, France, Canada, India, and Brazil.

Bhabha naturally became India's representative to the SAC. His selection was both unexpected and fortuitous. In December 1954, during his Christmas holiday in Bangalore, Bhabha received a phone call upon arrival at the airport, conveying Nehru's request for him to represent India at the SAC. Consequently, in January 1955, Bhabha travelled to New York to partake in the SAC's inaugural meeting.

Bhabha delivered an insightful address delving into the history of mankind's ceaseless quest for energy sources. While the discourse primarily centred around atomic fission, he dared to venture into the territory of fusion energy, making an audacious prediction about its potential. In the context of fusion, he elaborated on the process where two nuclei fuse together, leading to the release of energy. This mechanism, notably employed in a hydrogen bomb, required controlled containment for energy production. He underscored the inherent secrecy surrounding fusion research, surpassing even that of fission exploration. Expressing his visionary perspective, Bhabha posited, "The current epoch, where atomic energy generated by fission processes will partially cater to the world's power needs, might one day be recognised as the primitive phase of the Atomic Age."

Anticipating the potential of atomic energy via a fusion process, akin to that witnessed in hydrogen bombs, he held firm that existing scientific knowledge did not preclude the controlled procurement of this energy through fusion. He acknowledged the immense technical challenges but forecasted that within the upcoming two decades, a method to harness fusion energy under controlled circumstances would materialise. According to his projections, this achievement would pave the way for a brief respite in addressing the world's energy crisis, as the primary fuel required would be as abundant as the heavy hydrogen found in the Earth's oceans.

Regrettably, Bhabha's visionary forecast has yet to be realised. Despite extensive research efforts in the field of fusion energy, this vision remains elusive. His address, however, delivered a startling revelation to nations engaged in fusion research. Termed "Operation tin-opener" by Patrick Blackett, it drew attention to countries reticent to publicly discuss fusion. Both the USA and the UK confessed to their fusion research initiatives but maintained that its realisation was many years away. These statements were influenced by multiple factors. Industrial interests sought involvement in the profitable fission reactor industry and thus required assurances that fission reactors wouldn't become obsolete in the near future. Cockcroft criticised Bhabha's boldness, stating that a theoretical physicist might not comprehend the practical challenges as well as an experimental physicist would. Simultaneously, the British Association of Scientific Workers acknowledged Bhabha's forceful initiative in introducing this contentious subject matter to the Conference.

Within the conference, there emerged a sentiment that nuclear technology was an expenditure that economically underdeveloped nations like India should defer until they attained developed status. In contrast, Bhabha argued that India's vast population necessitated an immense energy supply, a` demand unattainable by fossil fuel reserves. The exorbitant cost of fossil fuel transportation reinforced his argument for atomic reactors, stating that nuclear-powered stations could potentially be more cost-effective than thermal power stations situated a considerable distance away from India's coal resources. These profound arguments showcased Bhabha's compelling advocacy in favour of atomic reactors.

There was a time when Nehru wanted a change in name for TIFR and that is another great story to hear about.

During the time of the foundation stone-laying ceremony, an intriguing narrative unfolded at TIFR, involving a moment where Nehru hesitated over the institute's name. This indecision was not mere coincidence. Bhabha had faced substantial pressure to rename the institute the prior year, with at least five alternative titles under consideration. The phrase "National" was a common inclusion in the names of many laboratories. The political atmosphere at the time signified the intricate balance between public funding and private influence in establishing a scientific institution. It was evident that governmental backing arrived with certain expectations. The association with the Tata name had been prevalent from the institute's inception. However, when the Institute was nine years old, Bhabha firmly opposed any alteration to its name.

In a persuasive argument, Bhabha highlighted the institute's established international reputation in both physics and mathematics. He referenced the accolades from Mexican physicist Manuel Vallarta, who hailed the work using nuclear emulsion techniques as the standout feature of the Bagneres Conference in 1953. The mathematics division had gained significant global recognition, often referred to as the "Princeton of the East."

At one point, Bhabha had discussed the name change with JRD Tata, albeit for different reasons. He sought intellectual freedom for the institute, including the liberty to engage with peace movements or attend Moscow delegations. These activities were a source of discomfort for the Tatas, given their connections with American businesses.

In his note on the institute's history in 1954, Bhabha argued that the institute had reached a stage where scholars, students, and academics from various corners of the world, including England, Israel, Japan, and the US, were eager to work there. He emphasised that changing the name would create unnecessary confusion unless compelling reasons warranted it. Bhabha reiterated that the institute's association with the business house should not detract from its national character or its eligibility for government funds. He even contemplated adding a secondary title to reflect its primary status and government affiliation, suggesting phrases like National Research Centre or National Research Institute. At the foundation stone-laying ceremony, Bhabha emphasised the need for distinct institutional identity, setting TIFR apart from national laboratories and university departments, emphasising its supreme position in scientific research in India.

Bhabha expressed gratitude to Nehru for laying the foundation stone and acknowledged the encouragement it provided to the staff. Shortly after this ceremony, Bhabha received an honour, being recognised in the honours list released on Republic Day. The Padma awards were established that year, honouring scientists prominently, with Raman among three recipients of the Bharat Ratna, and SN Bose among six recipients of the Padma Vibhushan. Bhabha himself was awarded the Padma Bhushan alongside Bhatnagar, JC Bose, and KS Krishnan.

Homi Bhabha, an eminent physicist and a significant figure in India's scientific landscape, found himself both a Nobel Prize nominee and a nominator during his illustrious career. While he was nominated for the prestigious prize five times by the esteemed French mathematician Jacques Hadamard between 1951 and 1956, Bhabha never secured the award. Hadamard's nominations, however, lacked compelling evidence, which led to their dismissal.

In the 1951 nominations, the Nobel committee acknowledged Bhabha's important contributions to cosmic radiation but was unable to recommend him for the prize due to insufficient reasoning provided by Hadamard. Subsequent nominations in 1953, 1954, 1955, and 1956 faced similar fates, as no new developments emerged to alter the committee's previous conclusions. Hadamard's brief letters of nomination failed to effectively advocate for Bhabha's candidacy, which weakened their impact.

It's notable that Hadamard, by then a seasoned serial nominator, had presented a considerable number of nominations for physics and chemistry in the first half of the 20th century, indicating his familiarity with the nomination process. However, his proposals for Bhabha, which appeared half-hearted, might be attributed to his age. At 85 years old during his initial nomination of Bhabha, Hadamard might have lacked the energy and robustness to write comprehensive proposals with supporting evidence.

Notably, like Bhabha, CV Raman, another revered Indian physicist, did not vigorously pursue the Nobel Prize. Raman, known for the Raman Effect, published numerous papers and corresponded with leading scientists. His nomination for the 1930 prize was backed by Rutherford and CTR Wilson, who provided an extensive list containing 160 papers. Rutherford even sought the assistance of Bohr in nominating Raman.

The Nobel nomination process involves drawing up a list of valid candidates after receiving nominations and expert group reports evaluating the contributions of these candidates. A shortlist is then compiled, with detailed reviews of potential candidates. Despite being nominated, Bhabha never made it to the shortlist, and consequently, no comprehensive report outlining his achievements was composed.

During the proceedings at Geneva, the Indian media followed the events with pride and admiration. Shankar's Weekly, an Indian counterpart to the satirical British magazine Punch, hailed Bhabha as the "Man of the Week" during the conference. The publication attributed considerable significance to Bhabha's contribution to the atoms for peace conference, foreseeing a transformative "Bhabha Effect" that would potentially enhance the lives of the Indian populace. The esteemed weekly expressed this notion, declaring that while the "Raman Effect" in pure physics had achieved its deserved acclaim, the prospect of a "Bhabha Effect" would mark a future advancement in improving the quality of life for the Indian people.

Upon his return, Bhabha dived headlong into the initiatives at Trombay. The construction of APSARA, India's pioneering nuclear reactor, had commenced. APSARA was a revolutionary swimming pool-type reactor utilising light water and enriched uranium. In 1955, an agreement was reached with the UK for the supply of enriched uranium. Despite this foreign collaboration, the reactor's design and all other aspects were entirely Indian. The final stages of the construction witnessed an intensive flurry of activities, with scientists and engineers toiling ceaselessly, culminating in Bhabha personally spending 48 continuous hours overseeing the last phase. Finally, in August 1956, APSARA achieved criticality.

This monumental achievement marked a milestone not only in bolstering India's self-assurance but also in facilitating studies across various fields, including radiation chemistry, biology, and the production of radioisotopes for agricultural research. As articulated by Greenstein, most European nations procured their reactors from the United States, whereas India accomplished the feat of building its reactor.

In January 1957, Nehru formally dedicated the reactor, christening it "APSARA." During the dedication speech, Nehru juxtaposed the historical significance of Elephanta Caves with the contemporary vision of Trombay's structures, representing a temporal bridge from Elephanta's ancient marvels to the modern advancements at Trombay, a quintessential mid-20th-century edifice.

Concurrently, the AEET campus in Trombay was also officially inaugurated. Bhabha, with a discerning eye for architecture's influence on society, emphasised the campus design's significance in a letter to Nehru. He expressed dissatisfaction with the standard practice of relying on the Central Public Works Department for government buildings, advocating for more architectural input, inspired by India's architectural legacy.

Bhabha's influence on the architectural endeavours extended to landscaping and horticulture. Not only was he deeply involved in the architectural planning, but he also paid attention to garden layouts. He is credited with initiating rose cultivation in Bombay, successfully growing numerous rose varieties in the Rose Garden within the AEET campus. His initiatives even extended to the afforestation of the Trombay hills.

In 1955, the Canadian government offered to assist India in constructing an NRX-type research reactor using natural uranium and heavy water as a moderator. Bhabha saw value in this offer, particularly because of the reactor's capability to produce plutonium, beneficial for India's second stage of nuclear development. To expedite communications, he believed it was better for this initiative to be within the scope of the Colombo Plan, despite initial obstacles in defining its parameters under the Commonwealth framework.

Bhabha quickly apprised Nehru of the Canadian offer while still in Geneva after the conference, seeking approval. Within three days, Nehru gave his consent, underscoring the rapid decision-making that propelled India's nuclear ambitions.

In 1956, construction began on the CIRUS (Canada-India Reactor Utility Services) located adjacent to APSARA. Bhabha advocated for the indigenous production of fuel elements, drawing from India's experience in manufacturing metallic uranium. When Canadian engineers expressed concerns about India's capability in this area, Bhabha took a bold step. He decided to dispatch two Indian-made fuel elements to Canada for a year-long trial in their NRX reactor at Chalk River to validate their performance. The successful performance of these elements in Canada significantly impressed the Canadian engineers, earning their respect. Throughout these developments, Bhabha kept Nehru apprised, detailing the progress and the enthusiastic efforts of the scientific staff, indicating the promising potential to satisfactorily produce fuel elements.

CIRUS became operational in the middle of 1959. Bhabha's foresight in building such a reactor in India served multiple purposes, including the training of Indian scientists and engineers. Recognising the need for specialised training instead of learning by doing, Bhabha established a training school to provide intensive courses for a year before deploying the trained recruits to designated sections of AEET. This strategic move aligned with Bhabha's vision of India grooming its own experts in nuclear energy within its boundaries, negating the necessity to seek expertise from abroad.

The selection for the school was solely merit-based, resulting in the enrolment of over 200 students each year. The success of this initiative, providing quality education to bright students from remote regions, made it a model for other educational institutions in India. The successful graduates were absorbed into AEET with competitive remuneration, comparable to the Indian Administrative Service (IAS) cadres, rendering this initiative one of the most successful programmes in India.

Apart from focusing on academic and technical training, Bhabha was attentive to grooming the students in decorum and etiquette to ensure they felt comfortable engaging in discussions with their international counterparts or while representing India overseas. As an experienced scientist-diplomat, Bhabha understood the nuances of international negotiations, assigning Western officers at AEET to oversee these aspects, ensuring a sense of professionalism and adherence to etiquettes among students. Bhabha's attention to detail extended to his regular visits to the student hostel for dinner, emphasising the importance of adhering to a dress code by requiring students to wear a trouser and a shirt or a tie in his presence.

Following the success of APSARA and CIRUS, the third reactor planned by Bhabha was a fully indigenous one named ZERLINA, aimed at research and the study of various fuel assemblies and lattice configurations. ZERLINA achieved criticality in January 1961.

Transitioning from research-focused reactors, Bhabha aimed to emphasise atomic reactors' viability for power generation and affordability. Through a global tender, the contract for the first project at Tarapur was awarded to General Electric of the USA. The project, referred to as a turnkey project, involved Indian personnel's significant participation, from site selection to the review of detailed designs, showcasing India's proactive role in the project. The negotiations for safeguards on equipment were challenging, with Bhabha asserting that safeguards should not apply unless they concerned special materials provided or produced at the reactor. Ultimately, a compromise was reached, respecting both stances, a testament to Bhabha's skills as a scientist-diplomat.

The negotiations reflected varying viewpoints and prolonged discussions between Joseph Wiesner and Bhabha. While Wiesner favoured the supervision of the IAEA for the power reactor, Bhabha supported a bilateral arrangement, representing India's preference for a unique leadership role rather than a perceived second-class position in the international nuclear realm. Wiesner acknowledged Bhabha's alignment with Nehru's aspirations, even when not comprehensively understood, acknowledging Bhabha's pro-Indian stance over perceptions of anti-American sentiments.

Bhabha's vision extended to the Tarapur Project, involving two 200 MW reactors powered by enriched uranium and light water. Concurrently, the plan for a heavy water power station in Kota, Rajasthan, was set in motion. This project aimed to have two 220 MW reactors, a joint endeavour with Canada. Recognising that these collaborations were insufficient for

India's goal of complete self-sufficiency, Bhabha outlined plans for a wholly indigenous reactor to be established and managed by India. This proposed a third atomic power station at Kalpakkam in Tamil Nadu, conceptualized in 1965, mere months before Bhabha's untimely passing.

Understanding the necessity for heavy water in powering these reactors, Bhabha orchestrated the establishment of the inaugural heavy water plant. He effectively persuaded the public-sector Fertilizer Corporation of India to integrate a heavy water production unit into the Nangal Fertilizer Plant, realised in 1962. Presently, India stands as one of the foremost producers of heavy water globally, boasting seven operational heavy water plants across the country.

Another significant initiative spearheaded by Bhabha was the construction of a reactor in Trombay dedicated to the separation of plutonium from irradiated fuel. This reactor, inaugurated by Lal Bahadur Shastri in January 1965, represented a significant stride in India's nuclear pursuits under Bhabha's guidance.

❑

What Changed With the Bomb?

The dropping of the atomic bombs on Japan, namely "Little Boy" on Hiroshima on 6 August 1945, and "Fat Man" on Nagasaki on 9 August 1945, had catastrophic consequences, claiming the lives of at least 70,000 and 35,000 residents, respectively. The use of these bombs raises significant questions about the moral and ethical justifications for such a devastating act. At the time of the atomic bombs' deployment, Germany had already surrendered, and the Japanese surrender quickly followed, effectively ending World War II.

There has been extensive discourse and research on whether the bombing of Japan was warranted. The prevailing conclusion from a vast body of literature suggests that Japan might have surrendered even without the use of nuclear weapons. The bombings provoked global unease and a sense of disapproval. Renowned physicist Albert Einstein, who was instrumental in alerting the US government about the potential development of nuclear weapons, expressed deep disturbance at the consequences of the bombings. He admitted to his secretary that had he known the Germans would not succeed in creating an atomic bomb, he would have refrained from getting involved in the process.

When India's first Prime Minister, Jawaharlal Nehru, shared his concerns about these events with Bhabha, Bhabha acknowledged the immense power that had been harnessed through fundamental physics research, despite its purely scientific origins. Bhabha argued that such research, while initially focused on theoretical and experimental progress, eventually led to practical applications and innovations. About four months following the events of the bombings, Bhabha initiated the Tata Institute of Fundamental Research (TIFR) in Bombay.

The atomic bombings of Japan cast a profound shadow over the world, sparking introspection, ethical considerations, and a re-evaluation of the implications of scientific advancements in warfare and humanity's well-being.

*****

Nuclear physics emerged as a pioneering area of scientific exploration in the early 1930s, captivating the attention of scientists globally, and Indian scientists were eager to engage in this emerging field. Radioactivity had already piqued the curiosity of early Indian scientists. Notably, Ruchi Ram Sahni, who had studied under Ernest Rutherford at Manchester University from 1912 to 1914, was among the first to delve into research on this subject while teaching at Forman Christian College in Lahore. As nuclear physics continued to develop as a burgeoning field, more Indian scientists joined the exploration. Some of these researchers included SN Bose from the University of Dhaka, who had associated with Marie Curie in Paris between 1924 and 1925, and Rajendra Lal De, also from Dhaka, who had worked with both Curie and Otto Hahn in Berlin. DM Bose, who initially worked at the Cavendish Laboratory and later with Erich

Regener in Berlin in 1919, was another physicist contributing to the advancements.

In 1948, the concept of becoming a nuclear power was not within the global purview. However, India, having recently gained independence, had a pool of highly skilled physicists who not only comprehended the significance of nuclear physics but also recognised the need for India to initiate an atomic energy programme as a national priority. Scientists like Bhabha, Meghnad Saha, and SS Bhatnagar were advocates of an Indian atomic energy programme and emphasised the imperative need to establish the capabilities required for pursuing nuclear physics in India. They recognised the significance of contributing to research in leading laboratories across Europe and the United States. Institutions such as the Cavendish Laboratory and the Radiation Laboratory at the University of California, Berkeley, with its remarkable work on the cyclotron, were pivotal for global advancements in this field.

Saha's interest in nuclear physics dated back to 1933, when he endeavoured to put forth a theory of beta decay with his student Daulat Singh Kothari, preceding Enrico Fermi's renowned theory on the same subject. In 1936, during his time in Allahabad, Saha was awarded a grant by the Carnegie Foundation, which facilitated his visit to Europe and the US He explored the Radiation Laboratory at the University of California, Berkeley, and met Ernest Lawrence, leaving him deeply impressed with Lawrence's cyclotron and its potential in nuclear research and medical treatment. Attending Niels Bohr's conference on nuclear physics in Copenhagen further expanded his insights. At the same conference, Bhabha was also present, possibly marking the first meeting between the two. Niels Bohr's institute in Copenhagen was in the early stages of constructing a cyclotron with funding from the Rockefeller Foundation.

Returning from his travels, Saha shared his insights from the conference in Science and Culture, his platform for discussing atomic energy and national scientific issues. He visited Princeton and met Milton White, overseeing the cyclotron, sparking an intense interest in the device. He was determined to construct a cyclotron in his laboratory, recognising it as a means to advance scientific infrastructure and elevate the stature of his institution. During this period, Saha learned that Arthur Compton of Chicago University, supported by Paul Langevin at the College de France, had nominated him for the Nobel Prize. Saha reached out to Niels Bohr, seeking support for his nomination. While he did not win the Nobel Prize, his credibility within the international physics community reached unprecedented heights.

The revelation of nuclear fission accelerated the global study of nuclear physics. Addressing the Indian Physical Society in March 1941, Saha underscored the discovery's transformative potential in energy production, remarking on its profound impact. He recognised the potential of a chain reaction but emphasised the need for empirical experiments to validate its practicability. His foresight extended to the idea of explosions in fissile material. Remarkably, this was articulated four years before his visit to North America and his exploration of sites linked with the Manhattan Project. It was also long before he suspected that significant work involving uranium-235 was already underway.

By 1939, the news of nuclear fission had spread across the scientific community, and notable figures like Saha, Bhatnagar, and Bhabha were in India, having returned from various places. They may have read about nuclear fission in articles such as those in Nature, enabling them to comprehend its theoretical underpinnings and the experimental requisites. While it's uncertain whether these three scientists discussed fission, a freeze on fission publications, imposed by Patrick Blackett in London from 1940 onward, hindered the dissemination of scientific details to benefit Germany. This information was part of the commencement of the race to construct the first nuclear weapon, which the Allies wished to keep under wraps.

Saha and Bhabha had an inkling that secretive efforts were underway, supported by an incident in 1942 involving Georgii Flerov, a Russian physicist who noted the absence of articles on fission in American journals and the lack of response to his collaborative work on the same topic.

Recalling events, Govind Swarup recounts Bhabha sharing that by 1944, he became convinced that the Americans had initiated a nuclear weapons programme. Bhabha's conviction stemmed from his correspondence with physicists worldwide during the war. His letters from colleagues in the US were subject to significant delays due to the war and distance, and these communications had substantially dwindled by 1943. Initially attributing the delay to the wartime situation, by 1944, Bhabha, having written several letters without any response, compiled a list of potential candidates for a nuclear programme. Astonishingly, the roster of his silent correspondents almost matched this list. This puzzling silence from key colleagues further reinforced his suspicion that a clandestine project was indeed in progress.

The aftermath of the bombing of Japan led to the realisation and alignment of the suspicions and fragmented information held by Indian scientists. A month following the bombing, Saha co-authored an account titled "The Story of the Atomic Bomb" for Science and Culture alongside BD Nagchaudhuri. Saha was conscious of the moral dilemmas arising from atomic bombs. He used an editorial in Science and Culture, in September 1945, to challenge the justifications made by Allied statesmen who claimed that the atomic bomb had saved lives by ending the war prematurely. Drawing an analogy to Genghis Khan's actions in Balkh, Saha vehemently criticised the rationale presented by the Allied leaders. He concluded on a hopeful note, expressing his confidence that scientific progress would address issues of reconstruction and significantly condense centuries of neglect into a few decades.

Subsequently, Saha summarised Henry DeWolfe Smyth's report, commissioned by Major General Leslie Groves, on the American involvement in the Manhattan Project. Smyth, a Princeton University physicist, aimed to elucidate key concepts to the public. Surprisingly, the report became a New York Times bestseller, persisting on the list for numerous months. Additionally, Saha contributed his article "The Atom Bomb" in the June 1946 edition of Science and Culture, providing details on the creation of an atomic bomb and the methods used for uranium separation.

In the pre-Independence era, planning surfaced as the medium through which Indian aspirations were articulated. Observing Japan's development following the Meiji Restoration and the rapid progress of the USSR through its initial five-year plan, many in India viewed planning as the ideal path toward national progress and development.

In October 1938, the idea of establishing the National Planning Committee (NPC) began to take shape in India. Initially, the committee was chaired by M. Visvesvaraya, an engineer-technocrat and the diwan of Mysore. Visvesvaraya was renowned for his writings on Indian reconstruction, and his book "Planned Economy for India" was published in 1934. However, scientists like Meghnad Saha and leaders like Subhas Chandra Bose believed that the NPC needed a prominent political leader as its chairman to gain the visibility and momentum it required.

Both Saha and Subhas Chandra Bose wrote to Jawaharlal Nehru, who was in London at the time, offering him the role of chairman for the NPC. Upon his return in November 1938, Nehru accepted the position, and Visvesvaraya stepped down. Saha was particularly convinced that Nehru was the right person to lead the NPC, as his leadership would symbolise broad support for industrialisation planning, ensuring its effective implementation. Additionally, Nehru's acceptance of the role would provide a science-based foundation for India's industrialisation efforts.

The NPC, under Nehru's leadership and managed by economist K.T. Shah, consisted of 15 members, including industrialists, scientists, economists, and a sceptical Gandhian, J.C. Kumarappa. The committee's office was located in various places in Bombay, including the Bombay University building. After World War II, JRD Tata provided space for the NPC in the New India Assurance Building.

Both Saha and Subhas Chandra Bose supported the idea that economic planning in India should prioritize industrialisation. They believed that the country's rapid industrialisation required an emphasis on industrial management and technical advancements. Saha, in particular, was critical of Mahatma Gandhi's emphasis on khadi (hand-spun cloth) and supported Subhas Chandra Bose's vision of swift industrial progress.

During the war, Saha played a crucial role in coordinating information related to India's capacity to produce steel products for wartime needs. His responsibilities extended to areas like scientific and technological education, cement and textile industries, and insurance and banking. He served on the boards of numerous scientific organisations.

The CSIR was established in September 1942, with S.S. Bhatnagar as its director. Saha and Bhatnagar had pivotal roles in coordinating scientific and industrial efforts during this period. While the CSIR was instrumental in promoting science-based industrialisation, it primarily served the war effort and the interests of British India.

Bhatnagar was in regular contact with key individuals responsible for India's industrial development, including Mudaliar, Dalal, and Sir Azizul Haque. He initiated projects aimed at replacing imported materials and skills with Indian alternatives, particularly in industries like textiles, steel, glass, and oil. The goal was to encourage indigenous production and reduce dependency on imports, fostering technical innovation and university research. However, both the BSIR and later the CSIR primarily served the war efforts during their initial years, rather than being oriented toward national development. Their main focus was to safeguard the interests of British India.

*****

The Nehruvian vision of science as an indispensable component of a modern society was a defining feature of independent India. Nuclear power held a special allure for leaders like Nehru due to its versatile potential: it promised to bring about material advancement by providing affordable electricity and also harboured the capability for developing the most powerful weaponry. Moreover, it symbolised scientific advancement and offered access to cutting-edge technologies.

Homi Bhabha, appointed as the chairman of the Board of Research in Atomic Energy under the CSIR, aspired beyond the limitations of institutional structures. His ambition and independence set him apart. He sought to create his own independent organisation for atomic research. In a concise note to Nehru in April 1948, titled "Note on the Organization of Atomic Research in India," Bhabha adeptly covered critical aspects concerning the organisation of atomic energy in the country. As noted by Itty Abraham, this note highlighted themes typical of the global growth of atomic energy programmes: elements such as secrecy, centralised authority, and executive autonomy.

Upon India's independence, Bhabha embarked on seeking external resources and expertise. He approached several countries, including France, the UK, and Canada. Although Nehru was initially hesitant to officially engage with foreign governments at that stage, he provided Bhabha with a cautious letter of reference. Bhabha had previously expressed his willingness to represent the Indian government while travelling in the US and Europe. His efforts bore fruit during a trip that included visits to France and Canada. Bhabha secured promises of uranium oxide from the

Canadians and the French agreed to aid in training scientists, sharing scientific knowledge, and constructing a factory for fissile material extraction in Travancore. His interactions during this visit provided insight into the progress made by these nations, leading him to believe that India was not far behind in this domain.

Homi Bhabha, upon his return from a foreign trip that included France and Canada, shared a detailed report with Nehru and engaged in discussions with Defence Minister Baldev Singh. The subject of defence was a major focus of attention for all involved. Nehru then tasked Baldev Singh with forming a scientific advisory committee and appointing Bhabha as one of its members. This led to the establishment of the Scientific Advisory Committee to the Ministry of Defence on 16 July 1948, which initially included members such as Bhabha, SS Bhatnagar, KS Krishnan, and later, DS Kothari as a scientific adviser to the Ministry of Defence. This committee was later renamed the Defence Science Advisory Board.

Concurrently, the Atomic Energy Bill was introduced by Nehru before the Constituent Assembly in early April 1948. Its main aim was to create an Atomic Energy Commission and lay the legal framework for its operation. The focus of debate largely revolved around the issue of secrecy. The Act proposed was more restrictive compared to the British or American legislations, emphasising complete secrecy in research and putting government control over all fissile materials necessary for atomic energy, notably uranium and thorium.

Nehru explained that the stringent secrecy was intended to safeguard Indian materials and knowledge from exploitation by "industrialised countries in a colonial manner" and to ensure that any foreign powers willing to collaborate with India could trust their secrets were safe. However, the Bill received criticism, particularly due to its secrecy provisions that didn't allow any legislative oversight. SV Krishnamurthy Rao voiced concerns about the excessive secrecy, questioning why peaceful uses were subject to such stringent secrecy when more advanced countries did not have such restrictions. Nehru had to acknowledge the interconnectedness between the secrecy and the defence-related aspects of the atomic energy project.

During the debates, Nehru admitted his inability to distinguish between peaceful and defence purposes concerning atomic energy. He acknowledged that the technology could serve both military and economic purposes, similar to the situations in the UK and the US. The passing of the Bill, even with minor amendments, recognised that atomic technology was inherently dual-purpose and inherently linked to national defence. This association helped support the provisions of the Bill, making concerns about secrecy somewhat redundant.

The Atomic Energy Board, following the conclusion of the debates, passed a resolution urging the government to set up a nuclear reactor (atomic pile) and allocate funds for capital equipment and research. It emphasised the need for heavy water capabilities and centralising the results of all surveys for atomic materials under the board, taking into account the essentiality of maintaining secrecy.

In his note to Nehru on 26 April 1948, Homi Bhabha highlighted two key points that needed consideration in organising the new organisation for atomic energy. First, he emphasised the necessity for absolute secrecy. Second, due to the limited availability of scientific and technical personnel, he suggested that some top scientists might need to undertake multiple roles concurrently. Bhabha proposed that the new organisation for atomic energy should be under the direct jurisdiction of the Prime Minister rather than being part of the Department of Scientific and Industrial Research.

He pointed out the inadequacy of entrusting the work to the existing Board of Research on Atomic Energy, which was an advisory body reporting to the governing council of the CSIR, consisting of 28 members. Bhabha believed the structure of the CSIR's atomic energy committee was impractical due to the diverse composition of its members, which included not only scientists and bureaucrats but also businessmen with varying scientific expertise. He convinced Nehru to establish a completely different structure for organising atomic energy.

Bhabha's request included setting up an independent secretariat for the AEC, allocating 1 crore over four years to the commission, and gaining approval to continue negotiations with France, the UK, and Norway under conditions of absolute secrecy. He intended to prepare complete bilateral agreements for government approval.

The success of establishing this new structure can be attributed to several factors. Bhabha's personal rapport with Nehru played a crucial role, as Nehru believed in Bhabha's capability to execute his vision for India's technological progress. Support from influential figures like the Tatas and SS Bhatnagar, a powerful technocrat, facilitated Bhabha's plans by countering resistance from other Indian scientists, particularly Ruchi Ram Sahni, who questioned the authority and resources granted to the AEC.

Bhatnagar responded to Bhabha's suggestions, indicating that he didn't want to obstruct Bhabha's efforts. Bhatnagar assured his support by acknowledging Bhabha's role and willingness to take a back seat, stating his preference to stay out of the conflict and expressing his confidence in Bhabha's capability.

This interaction revealed a respectful collaboration between Bhabha and Bhatnagar, with the latter expressing his support and assurance to not interfere with Bhabha's endeavours.

Bhatnagar's letter to Nehru indicated his agreement with Bhabha on most points, except for his own position. He advocated entrusting the entire work to Dr Bhabha, suggesting that Bhabha should take on the executive duties for the atomic energy work.

He expressed no hesitance to provide his service but believed that Bhabha should take the lead in the administration of atomic energy. This demonstrated Bhatnagar's willingness to support Bhabha's leadership in the atomic energy sphere.

On 5 May 5 1948, Bhabha wrote to John Cockcroft, inquiring about the administrative setup of the UK's atomic energy establishment. He sought details regarding the Telecommunications Research Establishment in Malvern to determine if it was an integral part of the atomic energy setup or simply developed suitable instruments for it. In addition, he requested designs for the magnet for the Wilson Chamber, acknowledging the potential difficulty in obtaining them but expressing his disappointment nonetheless.

Nehru, in a note to the cabinet on 22 May 1948, sought authorisation for the funds Bhabha had requested. He agreed with Bhabha on the need for secrecy and requested 1 crore to be allocated over a span of four years. Nehru also proposed the establishment of a heavy water plant and recommended that the AEC, envisioned as a small, high-powered body, report directly to the Prime Minister. Nehru's alignment with Bhabha's recommendations reflected his trust in Bhabha's capabilities and their strong rapport, marked by frequent personal interactions and mutual understanding.

The passing of the Atomic Energy Act on 10 August 1948, and the subsequent creation of the AEC under Bhabha's chairmanship, underscored the development of India's nuclear programme. Although the Act didn't explicitly mention the formation of a nuclear weapons structure, the language suggested that Bhabha harboured no doubt that India's nuclear programme would eventually serve a military objective.

The AEC's formation, with Bhabha as chairman, Bhatnagar, and KS Krishnan as its members, mirrored the scientific advisory committee to the Prime Minister. This marked the ascendancy of Bhabha as the leader of India's national nuclear establishment.

Notably, tensions arose between Bhatnagar, Saha, and SN Bose, reflecting divisions concerning their stance on Nehru's approach and the AEC.

Saha's attempt to rationalise his concerns by emphasising his reliance on Nehru's assistance indicated his awareness of the importance of maintaining Nehru's support. Saha pointed out his early acquaintance with Nehru, highlighting his interactions from a time when such affiliations weren't advantageous.

Bhabha's position was significantly bolstered, with Nehru and Bhabha establishing mechanisms to maintain complete control over the atomic energy programme. They crafted a setup where they led the programme without significant interference. The AEC reported directly to the Prime Minister's office, avoiding standard checks and balances, thereby securing substantial autonomy. This arrangement circumvented oversight from typical government mechanisms, allowing Nehru and Bhabha to maintain dominant control over the atomic energy initiative.

The role of Meghnad Saha in India's atomic energy narrative was marked by his significant disagreements with Homi Bhabha's vision and his subsequent exclusion from the AEC. Saha, despite his strong criticism of Bhabha's plans, was considered essential to the AEC. Nehru invited Saha twice to become a part of the commission, although Saha declined both times. He believed that India needed to concentrate on industrial growth and nuclear physics training within universities before initiating a comprehensive nuclear energy programme.

Saha criticised Bhabha's ideas, especially in the area of acquiring expertise from foreign nations. While Bhabha suggested importing first class personnel for experimental work in cosmic rays and nuclear physics, Saha prioritised developing local resources like mechanics, laboratory men, and engineering and manufacturing firms for scientific instruments. Saha's viewpoint emphasised the need for industrial growth and fostering regional scientific research centres affiliated with universities rather than central institutes controlled by the state. He advocated for self-sufficiency in technology to avoid dependency on foreign nations while strategically utilising international scholarly alliances for the country's advancement.

His refusal to join the AEC was seen as a crucial signal against Bhabha's plans, indicating his dissent despite not holding an official position. Saha's critiques of Bhabha's programme, often published in Science and Culture, were influential and informed journalists about India's nuclear programme. He remained informed about AEC developments through his network of former students and friends, ensuring that the public was aware of the nuclear programme's activities.

Saha's absence from critical AEC meetings limited his influence and ambitions in shaping nuclear policy. Despite his involvement in various projects and continued research in nuclear physics in Calcutta, Saha's broader engagement across multiple fields reduced his singular focus on organising for advancements in atomic energy.

Saha's exclusion from the AEC demonstrated a clash of visions between him and Bhabha on the strategic path for India's atomic energy and scientific research. Despite his significant contributions to the field of physics and his concerns about Bhabha's direction, Saha's involvement in the atomic energy programme remained limited due to his disagreements with the direction set by Bhabha and the AEC.

❏

What Happened in Geneva Conference and How Things Changed Afterwards

On 15 November 1945, post-World War II, the heads of the US, UK, and Canada met in Washington and collectively decided to enforce a veil of secrecy in the realm of nuclear energy, pending the establishment of a robust system for international oversight. The policy aimed to restrict the transmission of technical knowledge and uranium. Shortly after, in December of that year, the USSR consented to the creation of an atomic energy commission encompassing the 11 nations represented on the United Nations Security Council (UNSC), along with Canada. This proposal was approved by the UN on January 24, 1946.

In March 1946, David Lilienthal, who later became the inaugural chairman of the US AFC, was tasked with examining the challenges in developing nuclear energy for peaceful purposes. His report suggested centralising all activities concerning nuclear weaponry development under a single international authority. This envisioned body would oversee, operate, and advance the nuclear industry on behalf of all nations. It would have control over nuclear ores and fuels, conduct research, operate nuclear fuel fabrication facilities, and manage power reactors. International inspectors would monitor for any potential clandestine activities.

Presented at the first session of the United Nations Atomic Energy Commission (UNAEC) on 14 June 1946, by the US representative Bernard Baruch, the proposal became known as the Baruch Plan. The plan advocated the internationalisation of nuclear energy through an international atomic development authority, which would possess a monopoly over mining fissile materials such as uranium and thorium, processing ores, owning materials, and constructing and operating nuclear plants under the auspices of the UNAEC. However, the USSR rejected the Baruch Plan. Following this, the US established the Atomic Energy Act of 1946, enforcing a policy to obstruct the proliferation of nuclear technology through denial and secrecy. This even prohibited the sharing of information with US allies who had collaborated on the development of atomic bombs. If implemented, this would have impacted India as well. Bhabha opposed the US plans because they would entail international control over India's thorium and uranium reserves.

However, the negotiations turned fruitless, and after two years, the UNAEC reported to the UNSC that it had reached a deadlock and ceased its activities. The initial endeavours to achieve international nuclear disarmament fell short. From 1951 onward, discussions regarding nuclear controls were intertwined with traditional disarmament talks. There was a noticeable absence of any further discourse regarding the notion of international ownership and management.

The strategy of restriction ultimately proved ineffective, as the USSR conducted a successful test of a nuclear device as early as 1949, ending the United States' monopoly on nuclear capabilities. As a consequence, the Baruch Plan met an unobtrusive end. Meanwhile, the United Kingdom and France were making substantial progress, quickly catching up to the US and the USSR. Simultaneously, research on the peaceful applications of nuclear power, especially for commercial purposes, had been advancing steadily. By the close of 1953, it became evident that maintaining a policy of secrecy was relatively ineffective, prompting a sudden and significant change in the US approach.

The United States shifted from a stance of secrecy to actively advocating for the peaceful uses of atomic energy. This transformation was distinctly articulated in President Dwight Eisenhower's notable 'Atoms for Peace' speech, delivered before the United Nations General Assembly (UNGA) in December 1953, with Vijaya Lakshmi Pandit presiding. In his address, Eisenhower acknowledged the inevitability that other nations would acquire nuclear knowledge and emphasised the necessity of harnessing atomic energy for the betterment of society and progress. He specifically proposed that the primary nations involved in nuclear research and development contribute fissionable materials to establish an International Atomic Energy Agency (IAEA). This shift in the US policy marked a delayed realisation that the country's dominance in atomic energy had already been irrevocably lost.

The IAEA was to be established under the auspices of the United Nations, charged with the responsibility of safeguarding and preserving the fissionable materials provided by member states. The principal objective was to encourage the sharing of nuclear materials and technology for peaceful applications while simultaneously curbing the proliferation of nuclear weapons. This oversight was intended to be facilitated through an international agency that would monitor and regulate national nuclear programmes as mandated. In the words of President Eisenhower, the contributing nations would dedicate their capabilities to serving the needs, rather than the apprehensions, of humanity.

India faced numerous challenges regarding this proposition. Not all states were members of the United Nations, and several countries would likely resist external control over their nuclear programmes. Furthermore, there existed a pronounced disparity in nuclear knowledge among nations, with the smaller and recipient states consistently overshadowed by the major nuclear powers.

Following Eisenhower's address, the United States and the Soviet Union made concerted efforts to formulate a mutually agreeable plan for implementing these proposals. The United States, along with six other Western powers, advocated for the establishment of an international body to oversee and promote the development of atomic technology for peaceful purposes. The United Nations agreed to include this issue on the agenda of the United Nations General Assembly, and the Soviet Union appeared receptive to discussions on the matter. An instrumental aspect that facilitated negotiations with the USSR was the significant amendments made to the highly restrictive US Atomic Energy Act of 1946. These modifications were incorporated into the Atomic Energy Act of 1954, which included the relaxation of information classification on nuclear research, permitted private industry to own nuclear facilities and fissionable materials, and authorised the government to engage in cooperative agreements with other nations for the peaceful utilisation of nuclear energy.

In December 1954, a resolution was passed to convene an international technical conference under the United Nations' auspices by August 1955. The resolution mandated the invitation of all members of the UN and its specialised agencies to participate in the conference. A scientific advisory committee was established to craft the agenda and extend invitations. This committee comprised representatives from various nations, including Canada, Brazil, France, Britain, India, the USSR, and the US, with the UN Secretary General, Dag Hammarskjöld, presiding over the committee. India's representative in this committee was Bhabha, who was swiftly called upon to assume the role by Prime Minister Nehru, interrupting his holiday in Bangalore to travel to New York by mid-January 1955.

The geopolitical landscape shaped by the Cold War greatly influenced the proceedings from the outset. The composition of the committee itself mirrored the power dynamics of the global order. Representing the United States was Isidor Isaac Rabi, a Nobel laureate in physics and a physicist from Columbia University. Other committee members included W.B. Lewis from Canada, John Cockcroft from the UK, D.V. Skobeltsyn from the USSR, and Joaquim da Costa Ribeiro from Brazil. Bhabha was familiar with Lewis, Cockcroft, and the French representative, Bertrand Goldschmidt. Hammarskjöld's adeptness in articulating key points to achieve consensus and the personal acquaintances among most members, who were connected scientifically, facilitated their collaboration. Given the time constraints, much of the work was accomplished outside the formal committee sessions. Cockcroft recalls informal meetings, including a lunch at St. John's College, Cambridge, and subsequent sessions along the Norfolk coast, where initial groundwork was laid for drafting the conference programme. During a subsequent meeting in New York, Bhabha was unanimously elected as the conference chairman.

In February 1955, Bhabha received a letter from Frédéric Joliot-Curie, proposing an additional conference as a complement to the main event. Joliot-Curie suggested that this separate conference would highlight the dangers posed by atomic and thermonuclear weapons, expressing concern that exclusively focusing on the peaceful applications of atomic energy would overlook the prevailing global apprehension regarding atomic weapons.

The conference was scheduled to take place in Geneva from the 8–22 August 1955, selected to be held in the neutral territory of Switzerland to avoid objections from other countries. A major consideration revolved around choosing the conference president, a decision heavily influenced by geopolitical concerns. Initially, the United States advocated for a Swiss national to assume the presidency, but it was eventually agreed that a strictly non-partisan figure should hold the position. India, recognised as a potential nuclear state yet non-aligned, played a pivotal role in this process. Bhabha emerged as a universally acceptable choice, or at the very least, one that didn't provoke political objections, supported notably by the British delegation. Allegedly, Nehru also engaged VK Krishna Menon to actively advocate for Bhabha's candidacy. According to Laura Fermi, the official historian of the conference and Enrico Fermi's wife, it was Bertrand Goldschmidt, who had been involved in the Manhattan Project and later became an authority in nuclear policy, that proposed Bhabha's candidacy. Goldschmidt described Bhabha as an exceptional individual, a fusion of Eastern and refined intellectual traits, a person with a penchant for drawing, eloquent speech, and a deep passion for music.

Goldschmidt mentioned a fascinating anecdote—Bhabha's influence on the IAEA being headquartered in Vienna rather than Geneva. He attributed this choice to Bhabha's strong fondness for music. As Vienna is renowned for its musical heritage, especially the world-famous Vienna Philharmonic, Bhabha's desire to be more closely connected to the city was cited as a compelling reason for pushing the agency's base to be in Vienna, a decision that remains in place today.

Walter Whitman, a distinguished professor of chemical engineering at MIT, was appointed as the secretary general of the Geneva conference. The agenda and the official structure of the meeting were officially unveiled to the press by Hammarskjöld on February 1, 1955. Bhabha led the Indian delegation, which consisted of 24 members and supporting staff to Geneva. Among the delegates, KS Krishnan held the most senior position, accompanied by individuals like VR Khanolkar, the director of the Indian Cancer Research Centre, and the diplomat Arthur Lall. The remaining team comprised young nuclear physicists who would later play significant roles in India's nuclear programme, including AS Rao, Homi Sethna, KS Singwi, V.N. Meckoni, and KG Vohra.

The Institute of Nuclear Physics, seen as the only other reputable institution for nuclear physics research, was tasked with nominating delegates for the conference. Saha, a key figure at the Institute, recommended a list of scientists, which included BD Nagchaudhuri and his son Ajit Kumar Saha. However, Bhabha controversially excluded the Calcutta delegation by establishing an unsupportable distinction between nuclear technology and nuclear physics. He contended that the conference in Geneva was primarily focused on nuclear technology and energy, thus not aligning with the interests of nuclear physics researchers. Bhabha wielded considerable influence over matters of nuclear research, a power that required constant validation, maintenance, and enhancement. The composition of the Indian delegation to the Geneva conference was one such instance where Bhabha's authority was exhibited.

Although the exclusion of the Calcutta delegation appeared unsustainable based on the arguments Bhabha presented, his reasoning might have been motivated by specific reasons, potentially backed by support from Nehru.

In October 1954, during a conference in Moscow, Saha and DS Kothari, serving as delegates of the Government of India, had engaged in discussions regarding a reactor for the defence ministry. Driven by his enthusiasm, Saha sought permission to negotiate on behalf of the government. His eagerness was partly influenced by rumours he had heard during his visit to the United States earlier that year, suggesting US assistance to Pakistan with a reactor. Fearing India's exclusion as a friendly nation by the US, Saha believed that the country had better prospects with the USSR. However, unbeknownst to Saha, just a month before, Cockcroft had offered India designs for a nuclear reactor. The prospect of a deal with the USSR might have caused considerable embarrassment, which Bhabha sought to avert in Geneva by excluding the Calcutta delegation entirely.

Saha struggled to reconcile his diminished role and the constraints that prevented him from participating in international discussions or negotiations as an individual. Gone were the days when he could attend such events independently. This change was triggered by India's transition from a colony to a sovereign state, the increased utilisation of nuclear technology for developing weapons, and the influence of the Cold War. While Saha was aware of these factors, his aspirations for the Calcutta group, as well as his personal ambitions, propelled him to continue his efforts. Nonetheless, Bhabha's dominance over nuclear research was now absolute.

The conference in Geneva was a significant gathering, attracting 1,428 delegates from 73 nations and seven specialised UN agencies. It also accommodated an equal number of observers and approximately 900 media representatives, making it one of the most extensive scientific conferences held to date. The venue was the majestic Palais des Nations, the UN's residence in Geneva, offering stunning views of Lake Geneva. More than a thousand papers were presented for discussions. As Jahnavi Phalkey aptly noted, if the Empire Scientific Conference of 1946 was a plea to maintain imperial preference in post-war international politics, the Atoms for Peace conference in Geneva in August 1955 was an invitation to establish American preference (in competition with the USSR) in Cold War politics. The focal point of the American display was a swimming-pool-type research reactor, transported to Geneva and assembled during the conference.

At the Geneva conference, even President Eisenhower took a break to visit the American exhibit and view the reactor, underlining the monumental significance of this scientific gathering. Notably, a multitude of eminent scientists from around the world, with the notable exception of Albert Einstein, convened. This event marked a turning point in science and technology as these experts collectively resolved to make scientific knowledge accessible to the broader populace. Projects previously veiled in wartime secrecy were now openly discussed and shared, marking a moment of triumph for Bhabha.

Bhabha commenced the conference on 8 August 1955 with his presidential address, titled 'The Need for a New Power Source'. His speech, delivered with a ceremonial tone yet devoid of pretentiousness, aimed to discuss the peaceful utilisation of atomic energy and the exchange of scientific and technical knowledge on this critical subject.

Bhabha proposed a sweeping view of human history, dividing it into three distinct epochs, each characterised by a different primary energy source. The initial and lengthiest epoch, spanning nearly 250,000 years, relied on muscle power, be it human or animal. The subsequent epoch, emerging around 200 years ago, centred on the combustion of fossil fuels like coal and oil, ushering in the industrial society we witness today. Bhabha foresaw the third epoch as the age of atomic energy, which commenced after World War II. He envisioned that electricity derived from atomic reactors would play a pivotal role in fostering economic development.

Bhabha's assertion stemmed from the belief that economic progress and energy consumption are intrinsically intertwined. He highlighted the connection between energy supply and civilisation's development. In societies relying on the physical labour of slaves, the benefits of civilisation were exclusively reserved for an elite few. However, Bhabha believed that the increased supply of electricity, primarily from atomic energy, would be the linchpin for broader economic development, democratising the benefits of civilisation.

As part of his speech, Bhabha highlighted the significant disparity in living standards among different regions due to the unequal distribution of resources. He presented compelling figures regarding energy production and consumption rates, emphasising that if the entire world's population were to consume energy per capita at the same rate as the United States, the world's fossil fuel resources would be depleted in a notably brief period.

Focusing on the urgency of industrialising underdeveloped regions for the progression of civilisation, Bhabha emphatically stressed that atomic energy was not just a requisite but an absolute necessity. He underscored the indispensability of atomic energy for industrialisation and the continuation of civilisation's advancement. While he clarified that atomic weapons were beyond the scope of that particular conference, he articulated the interconnection between the peaceful applications of atomic energy and the menacing spectre of warfare. Bhabha asserted that the widespread use of atomic power worldwide would necessitate an international consensus among major powers to sustain global peace.

Drawing from the Russell-Einstein Manifesto issued on 9 July 1955, Bhabha echoed the caution against nuclear conflict and the earnest plea for global peace. The manifesto, authored by Bertrand Russell and Albert Einstein, sounded the alarm on the grave perils of nuclear weapons and called for robust efforts to avert such dangers. The consequential impact of this manifesto was evident in the convening of the inaugural Pugwash conference in 1957. The roots and objectives of this conference were deeply rooted in the manifesto's principles - emphasising the perils of nuclear weaponry, advocating for their eradication, and promoting the peaceful resolution of conflicts.

Nearly a decade prior to the Geneva conference, Albert Einstein, as chairman of the Emergency Committee of Atomic

Scientists, reached out to Bhabha in April 1947, seeking support for educating the public about atomic energy and its societal implications. Einstein and the committee believed that an informed citizenry was the key to promoting life over death in the realm of nuclear power. Bhabha assured Einstein of his wholehearted assistance, expressing eagerness to disseminate literature on the subject to a wider audience. However, due to stringent dollar restrictions imposed by the Indian government, providing financial aid was challenging for Bhabha at that time.

Bertrand Russell, reminiscing about the genesis of the manifesto, held strong aspirations for the endorsement of Indian leaders and scientists. His optimism soared as Jawaharlal Nehru commenced his visit to London in February 1955, displaying a deeply sympathetic and amicable demeanour, even inviting Russell to contemplate holding the maiden meeting of the manifesto in India. The prospect of the Indian government fostering what would ultimately evolve into the Pugwash conferences seemed promising. The choice of New Delhi as the inaugural conference site was on the horizon, and by June 1956, Russell had begun dispatching invitations for a slated conference in January 1957. However, Homi Bhabha's lukewarm reception of the Pugwash movement and his tepid enthusiasm for nuclear disarmament placed a damper on these anticipations. Bhabha seemed reluctant to align with what was perceived as a movement inspired by "fellow-travellers".

A face-to-face meeting between Russell and Bhabha painted a starkly different picture. Russell described the encounter as receiving a 'cold douche.' Bhabha's reservations about such a manifesto or the envisioned Pugwash conference became unmistakably clear. As Russell put it, there was minimal support forthcoming from the official scientific circles in India, as not a single Indian nuclear scientist endorsed the Russell-Einstein Manifesto. Despite this setback, the inaugural Pugwash conference convened in July 1957, taking place in Pugwash, Nova

Scotia, Canada, owing to the generous offer of Cyrus Eaton, an industrialist and benefactor who agreed to host and finance the gathering. There were other offers to host the conference, including one from the Greek shipping tycoon Aristotle Onassis, which was declined. On Russell's counsel, Nehru instituted an official committee to scrutinise the repercussions of nuclear explosions.

In his concluding remarks, Bhabha articulated a compelling argument for knowledge to be more openly shared and contradicted the notion that security could be assured through secrecy. He advocated for the accessibility and dissemination of knowledge, stating that relying on secrecy for security was a fallacy. Bhabha emphasised that true security could not be founded on concealing knowledge, promoting the idea of freely sharing information for the greater good. He expressed hope that the conference would contribute to advancing humanity towards an increasingly enlightened phase in the atomic era, promising a life that would be richer and happier than could be currently imagined.

Bhabha's inaugural address included two rather unexpected, and possibly contentious, statements. The first pertained to the absence of China from the conference due to its non-membership in the United Nations. Bhabha expressed his regret that parts of the world representing a quarter of the global population were not directly represented at the conference. Even though this was a scientific conference and political questions were deemed off-limits, Bhabha's reference to the absence of representation from certain regions garnered attention but was mostly disregarded. Bhabha's allusion may have been in alignment with Nehru's perspective, given Nehru's advocacy, as the leader of the non-aligned movement, for China's inclusion in the UN.

The other, more controversial statement was about fusion energy, made during the concluding portion of Bhabha's address. He remarked that the current stage, where atomic energy was generated through the fission process, might be viewed in the future as the rudimentary phase of the atomic era. Bhabha highlighted that although atomic energy was obtained through fission, there was no scientific basis to assert that controlled energy from the fusion process was unattainable. He boldly predicted that within the subsequent two decades, a method would be discovered to liberate fusion energy in a controlled manner. Bhabha expressed his confidence that this breakthrough would resolve the world's energy crisis, as the fuel, found abundantly in heavy hydrogen within the Earth's oceans, would be readily available.

Bhabha's optimism seemed to have led to an overestimation of the feasibility of fusion energy for resolving the energy crisis. However, his final remarks, centred on the emergence of an era marked by international cooperation in the realm of atomic energy, offered a promise of a brighter future for humanity. This vision of cooperative advancement held far greater significance.

Bhabha's profound statement about sharing knowledge for the collective benefit at the conference played a pivotal role. Fusion, although not officially on the conference's agenda and absent from the papers presented, was a highly classified subject under the extensive research of the US, UK, and USSR. Bhabha, having some awareness of this ongoing secret research, seemed motivated by an informed suspicion coupled with his discontent about the pervasive secrecy surrounding fusion research, prompting his unexpected mention of fusion during his address. His remarks on fusion at the conference were unconventional and marked a significant shift towards transparency.

This unexpected announcement struck a chord among many nations because multiple countries had clandestinely been involved in fusion research. Bhabha's public acknowledgement challenged the prevailing atmosphere of secrecy and veiled operations in the realm of fusion energy.

The repercussions of Bhabha's disclosure were particularly discomforting for the United States. Until then, Project Sherwood, the American programme for controlled nuclear fusion initiated during the Eisenhower administration, had been heavily shrouded in secrecy. Bhabha's move disrupted this silence, and the Americans were constrained in their ability to respond to Bhabha's speech. Raja Ramanna reflected that Bhabha aimed to shake the Americans out of their secretive approach. Some experts argue that Bhabha's bold declaration was the catalyst that prompted the initial steps toward the declassification of the fusion programme. The open presentation of scientific findings underscored the preliminary nature of existing knowledge and facilitated the trend toward the internationalisation of the field, reducing the prevailing sense of competition among nations.

Patrick Blackett described the occurrence as 'operation tin-opener,' suggesting that if the conference were presided over by a less assertive figure, the revelation of the potential of fusion might not have surfaced as it did. It is plausible that Bhabha's move was a calculated risk that reverberated within scientific and political circles.

Bhabha's ground-breaking statement, especially followed by the British acknowledgement, might have set the stage for an eventual American disclosure and a more transparent approach to the subject. This timely announcement indeed carried weight and likely had a lasting impact. Abdus Salam commented that the disclosure altered the perception of fusion, which until then was a closely guarded secret. He noted that Bhabha's speech led to a degree of declassification in the fusion domain, raising Bhabha's standing among the global scientific community. Post-conference, Bhabha gained increased respect in Indian political circles, cementing Nehru's confidence in his capabilities with an international endorsement.

The aftermath saw significant statements from key figures. Cockcroft expressed optimism that fusion power could be within reach in a generation. Admiral Lewis Strauss, chair of the US AEC, admitted the US's longstanding research on controlled thermonuclear reactions during a press conference. Bhabha, addressing the press, not only stood by his statements but also highlighted the continued relevance of fission power even in a future era of fusion power. Subsequently, Admiral Strauss, in a press briefing in Washington, revealed essential information about Project Sherwood.

Bhabha's pronouncement brought about concern among business delegates attending the conference. Fission power reactor entrepreneurs sought reassurance about the sustainability of their industry. Several fission power reactors were operational or under construction in countries like the US, UK, USSR, France, and Canada. The commercial exploitation of fission reactors had been a driving force behind the 'Atoms for Peace' initiative, where UK and US firms showed a keen interest in selling reactors and power stations to other nations. These discussions and negotiations were a significant backdrop to the formal conference proceedings.

John Cockcroft, leader of the British delegation, attempted to provide context to Bhabha's bold statement in his lecture on August 19, where he highlighted the contrasting approaches of experimental and theoretical physicists. In his remarks, Cockcroft acknowledged Bhabha's courage, indicating that as an experimental physicist, he had a more intricate understanding of the challenges involved in scientific pursuits.

In a retrospective assessment shortly after the conference, Cockcroft expressed his delight at the event's success. Writing in Nature, he noted that the conference had exceeded their expectations, uniting the East and West in the realm of physical sciences after a prolonged period of division. He emphasised that the conference served as a platform where numerous individuals from various parts of the globe came together as friends. Cockcroft observed that the conference played a significant role in re-establishing the standard mode of scientific communication and collaboration globally.

The gathering of delegates revealed that fundamental research in the field of nuclear sciences was progressing similarly across various nations and that the secrecy surrounding this research was ineffective in confining the spread of knowledge. It was evident that no single nation held absolute superiority, and the pre-war cosmopolitan scientific community, which had been nationalised during the conflict, was gradually returning to its more international, collaborative state. It was also apparent that none of the nations had made substantial progress towards effectively utilising atomic power for civilian energy production.

In correspondence to Nehru dated 24 August 1955, Bhabha delivered a comprehensive overview of the conference proceedings. According to Bhabha's report, the Indian delegation presented a total of 13 papers, well received by the attendees. Specifically, he highlighted his own paper discussing the pivotal role of atomic energy in India, notably referenced by Cockcroft in his evening lecture. Bhabha also detailed a significant contribution made by a young scientist, K.G. Vohra, involving a radical method for uranium surveying, which even gained mention in The New York Times.

Expressing an encouraging observation, Bhabha noted the apparent dissipation of Cold War tensions at the conference, indicating a favourable environment for expanded cooperation in the field of atomic energy. Stressing the importance of future endeavours, Bhabha emphasised the need for tact and discretion to ensure that any forthcoming actions in the field wouldn't detract from the positive psychological atmosphere that currently prevailed.

In a notable recognition of Bhabha's role, Shankar's Weekly, akin to the Indian version of Punch, honoured Bhabha as 'The Man of the Week' in its August 14 issue. The publication presented an intriguing paradox of the era, highlighting the choice between self-extermination or the creation of a world without limits to material prosperity. Specifically commending Dr. Bhabha, the magazine hailed him as India's foremost atomic scientist, lauding his unwavering commitment toward achieving a future brimming with endless material opportunities and rejecting the path of self-annihilation.

The Soviet delegation leader, Skobeltsyn, extended an invitation to Bhabha and the Indian contingent for a post-conference visit to the USSR. This planned visit was anticipated even before their departure for the Geneva conference. The groundwork for this visit had been established during Nehru's visit to the USSR in 1954, which played a significant role in fostering closer ties between the two nations.

Skobeltsyn was renowned for his contributions to cosmic ray research and was instrumental in advancing Russian investigations in this field. He was the first physicist to conduct experiments placing a Wilson Chamber within a magnetic field, a pioneering effort that confirmed cosmic rays as high-energy particles. Skobeltsyn led the initiation of cosmic ray research in key Russian cities like Leningrad and Moscow, cultivating a cohort of distinguished physicists specialising in cosmic ray studies.

Accompanied by a team consisting of KS Krishnan, Ramanna, N.S. Prasad, Sethna, and A.S. Rao, Bhabha embarked on their journey to Moscow on 30 August 30 1955, aboard an aged Ilyushin aircraft. Although the travel was characterised by its lengthy duration and the persisting noise, the warm reception upon their arrival in Moscow compensated for the inconvenience of the journey. Despite their late-night arrival, the Indian delegation was welcomed by esteemed members of the Soviet Union's Academy of Sciences. As recounted by Ramanna, they were received akin to a high-profile delegation, signifying the importance of the occasion. Krishnan diligently maintained a daily diary that provided invaluable insights into the detailed experiences and happenings during their visit.

The visit commenced on 1 September 1955, at the Institute of Scientific and Technical Information, providing the Indian delegation with a comprehensive exposure to a wide array of scientific and technical publications, along with abstracting services. The subsequent visit was to the Lebedev Institute of Physics in Moscow, an establishment directed by Skobeltsyn. This was succeeded by tours to a machine tools factory and Moscow University on the following day. On 3 September, the Indian delegation journeyed to the Institute of Nuclear Problems at Dubna, a small town located close to a substantial dam on the Volga, approximately 120 km away from Moscow. The focal point of the visit was the synchrocyclotron, which, at that time, stood as the largest of its kind in the world.

A leisurely Sunday allowed for some sightseeing before the delegation was taken to the site of the first Soviet-constructed natural uranium reactor on the subsequent day. This reactor's specifics had been presented during the Geneva Conference. The following day, the delegation visited the Institute of Physical Problems, where they had the opportunity to meet its director, the renowned Pyotr Kapitza, alongside esteemed members like Lev Landau and Evgeny Lifshitz. Kapitza, reuniting with Bhabha after an extended period, exhibited a turbine-operated liquid air plant capable of producing 200 litres of liquid air per hour. He informed Bhabha and Krishnan about the commissioning of a larger helium plant, anticipating that liquid helium would soon be as accessible as liquid air or nitrogen. Their discussions included Kapitza's work on superconductivity at the institute. Later that day, Bhabha and Krishnan engaged in an official meeting with Deputy Foreign Minister Vasili Kuznetzov.

The subsequent destination for the delegation was Leningrad, where they made a comprehensive visit to the Physico-Technical Institute of the USSR Academy, an establishment inaugurated by the distinguished Russian physicist Abraham Joffe. During the visit, Krishnan discovered that the group there was already well-versed with the National Physical Laboratory's (NPL) work on thermionics in New Delhi. The next visit was to the Academy of Sciences of the Soviet Union on September 10. The evening was dedicated to the enchantments of ballet, featuring a grand performance of Serge Lifar's Romeo and Juliet, starring the renowned ballerina Galina Ulanova. In the audience were notable figures, including Russian Premier Nikolai Bulganin and West German Chancellor Konrad Adenauer.

The journey continued with a trip to Voronezh, where the delegation had the opportunity to witness the construction of new nuclear reactors. Subsequently, they travelled to Zaporozhye, a city situated in Ukraine on the banks of the Dnieper River, renowned for its dam and a hydroelectric power station, built in 1932. The dam had faced destruction during the war but was meticulously reconstructed thereafter. The delegation was lodged in a guest house near the dam. Ramanna recollected a seemingly trivial yet amusing incident that transpired there. While the guest house provided many comforts, it appeared that there was a shortage of water and toilet paper. Bhabha requested Ramanna to seek some toilet paper from the kindly old caretaker. However, faced with a language barrier, Ramanna's attempts at sign language to convey the request were futile. The caretaker, lacking English proficiency, called someone who did, and upon understanding the request, returned with a heap of old copies of Pravda, a humorous and unintended outcome of the misunderstanding.

After concluding their extensive visits to Kiev and Sverdlovsk in the Arctic Circle, the delegation's two-week journey ended with a cordial farewell dinner hosted by the Academy in Moscow on 16 September. Subsequently, the delegation boarded a flight to Stockholm via Helsinki, where a special dinner was arranged at the residence of Professor Manne Siegbahn in honour of the visiting group. The following day marked a transitional phase as two members of the delegation, Krishnan and Sethna, departed for

London, leaving Bhabha and the remaining members to continue their discussions in Sweden. Remaining in Stockholm, Bhabha and Ramanna then flew to Canada to further explore discussions regarding the establishment of an NRX-type reactor in India. This new and notably cooperative approach from Canada was a marked departure from their previous reluctance to share details about the same reactor, evident only a year prior.

In the wake of the Geneva Conference, the USSR promptly expressed their interest in participating in the envisioned agency, advocating for the third draft statute, which the US government had composed in March 1955, as a foundational point for initiating discussions. Subsequent deliberations on the statute's final text took place during two distinct conferences held in Washington D.C. and New York in the early and late months of 1956, respectively. This process involved the participation of 12 countries highly engaged in establishing the new agency. The countries that had been consulted regarding the drafts of the statute were extended invitations, alongside the USSR, Czechoslovakia, Brazil, and India, to take part in the conference held in February and March 1956. This conference spanned four weeks and was marked by a conciliatory and accommodating approach adopted by the USSR. Consequently, the resultant organisation that emerged from these negotiations wielded significant supervisory powers, functioning more in the capacity of a mediator than a financial authority.

On 23 September 1956, the draft statute was introduced to a gathering of representatives from 81 nations at the UN headquarters, marking a critical turning point in the discussions. The crux of contention surrounded the expansive scope of safeguards, an issue that Bhabha, leading the Indian delegation, grappled with intensely. While Bhabha acknowledged certain safeguards related to enriched uranium and plutonium, he vehemently opposed applying safeguards to natural uranium. He was vocal about the inherent neo-colonial implications of stringent safeguards, emphasising that advanced nations with nuclear armament would not require the agency's assistance, leading to a stark division of nations into atomic "haves" and "have-nots" dominated by the agency.

Bhabha saw this division as a potential source of severe tensions, undermining the primary goal of safeguards to ensure a peaceful global environment. France, represented by Goldschmidt, supported Bhabha's stance, advocating for a relaxation of the rigorous safeguards on natural uranium. They stressed the importance of not imposing overly strict regulations that might dissuade potential member nations from seeking support from the agency in the future.

Bhabha's opposition to an enduring application of safeguards, especially concerning future generations of nuclear materials, was underlined by the looming scenario for India. India had nuclear materials but required aid to initiate a nuclear programme, positioning Bhabha at the forefront of India's campaign to dilute the scope of these safeguards. The draft statute dated September 10, 1956, proposed depositing plutonium and other special fissionable materials with the agency, with certain allowances for members to retain specified quantities for non-military use under supervision. Bhabha strongly rejected the agency's broad oversight over plutonium reprocessing and the possession of resulting plutonium, pressing for a more restrained approach.

In the deliberations held on September 27, 1956, Bhabha articulated a firm stance, advocating for the inherent right of states to generate and maintain the fissionable materials necessary for peaceful power programmes. However, Bhabha confronted a pertinent issue regarding the plutonium derived from foreign reactors, notably ones like CIRUS, and whether they should fall under the jurisdiction of the IAEA. Despite the negotiation of CIRUS predating the establishment of the IAEA and being subject only to bilateral safeguards, future discussions involving foreign assistance would potentially come under the IAEA's oversight.

Bhabha emphasised the deceptive nature of stringent safeguards, highlighting the potential for any nuclear aid, including training and materials, to have military implications by enabling a country to redirect resources toward a military programme. To address this concern, Bhabha proposed a specific criterion for the new agency, suggesting that assistance should be extended only to nations without military programmes. He defined military programmes as those related to nuclear and thermonuclear explosives and radiological weaponry, excluding military nuclear propulsion.

He cautioned that some technically advanced states could engage in projects aided by the Agency, ostensibly abiding by the present safeguards, while simultaneously conducting their independent, unsupervised programmes. Bhabha voiced concerns that these countries might utilise the knowledge and expertise gained from the Agency-aided initiatives without being subject to any safeguard system.

Bhabha was staunch in his opposition to safeguards that could significantly impede India's three-stage nuclear energy programme, particularly hindering the acquisition of plutonium from spent fuel in natural uranium reactors. His argument revolved around the notion that imposing safeguards would practically prohibit the acquisition of plutonium, crucial to India's nuclear energy strategy.

Bhabha specifically objected to the broad authority granted to the new agency under Article XII.A.5. This clause conferred the agency with decision-making power over the use of all special fissionable materials obtained or produced in the process and mandated that such materials be deposited with the agency. This provision, allowing control over the fissionable materials, might have had far-reaching implications, potentially influencing a country's economic autonomy, particularly if its nuclear power generation, based on contributions from the new agency, had been foundational only in its initial stages.

Following the US delegation's refusal to significantly modify its stance even after consultations, the conference, which was nearing its end on 19 October 1956, faced the risk of a deadlock. At this juncture, the USSR, hitherto silent, aligned itself with India and its allies. Anticipating a potential impasse, Goldschmidt and Lindt intervened by proposing a compromise amendment. This amendment granted countries the right to retain specific quantities of self-produced fissionable materials for their research and nuclear reactor fuelling purposes.

After deliberations and influence from the Canadian delegation, the Franco-Swiss proposal was embraced, ultimately paving the way for the unanimous adoption of Article XII the next day. This outcome prevented a breakdown of the conference and resolved the last hurdle to establish the IAEA and its crucial safeguards, contributing to the current global policy of non-proliferation.

In the culmination of the negotiations, the final statute marked a significant departure from highly stringent safeguards. The recipient countries were allowed to possess plutonium derived from spent fuel in foreign-supplied nuclear reactors, using it for peaceful endeavours. Bhabha emphasised that the revised statute ensured that the fissionable material generated in Agency-aided projects within a country would be under that country's jurisdiction. This arrangement preserved the country's autonomy to decide the usage of such material, thereby preventing the agency from unduly interfering in the economic development and national life of the concerned states.

Bhabha was pragmatic in his understanding that the proposed safeguards by the IAEA wouldn't prevent countries from pursuing nuclear weapons programmes. He acknowledged the final statute, realising that India could benefit from international aid without compromising its nuclear weapon capability.

A humorous incident recounted by Cockcroft highlighted Bhabha's disregard for time. Known for his lack of punctuality,

Bhabha's tardiness at the IAEA meetings was a notable trait. According to Cockcroft, while Bhabha was punctual at the UN Scientific Advisory Committee sessions under Hammarskjöld's leadership, he often arrived late for other IAEA meetings. To address this, the secretary intentionally advertised the meeting's official time half an hour ahead, ensuring Bhabha's timely arrival and causing amusement among attendees.

Eisenhower's Atoms for Peace initiative led to a relaxation in the control over nuclear information. Both the US and the USSR rushed to declassify and distribute a significant volume of technical information. By 1958, the US made nearly all basic scientific knowledge in the field of nuclear fission accessible to any nation. However, the core predicament of how to prevent nuclear weapons' proliferation while promoting nuclear energy's benefits, considering their shared fundamental raw materials and technology, remained unsolved.

The second UN International Conference on the Peaceful Uses of Atomic Energy, held in September 1958 in Geneva, was a larger event compared to the inaugural conference. Although the technical presentations were abundant, the second conference lacked the striking impact of the first. This was partly due to the less optimistic outlook stemming from the realisation that nuclear power generated from fission energy wasn't as cost-effective as initially predicted. Notably, Francis Perrin of France was appointed to preside over the conference, with Sigvard Eklund of Sweden serving as its secretary general. It was also an honour for Sethna to be chosen as the deputy director general, signifying recognition of his standing. AS Rao was among the 25 secretaries appointed to prepare for and manage the various technical sessions of the conference.

A significant outcome of the first conference in 1955, during which Bhabha introduced the topic of fusion, was its inclusion in the agenda for the second Geneva conference. Bhabha was designated to preside over the plenary session discussing the

'Possibility of Controlled Fusion'. The conference, while highlighting the controlled fusion aspects, exercised caution in its predictions. Bhabha and WB Lewis presented a paper titled 'Canada-India Reactor: An Exercise in International Collaboration', an aspect further explored in a later chapter.

In addition to the general and technical sessions, the conference featured a series of six evening lectures by distinguished scientists. Bhabha inaugurated these lectures, speaking on 'Need for Nuclear Power in Underdeveloped Countries'. His discourse aimed to dispel the notion that atomic energy's immediate applications were confined to industrially advanced nations.

At the third conference held in September 1964, Bhabha presented a paper discussing 'World Energy Requirements and the Economics of Nuclear Power with Special Reference to Underdeveloped Countries'. In this paper, he estimated that nuclear power would generate two million MW of electricity worldwide by the year 2000. Bhabha's famous remark, 'No power is as expensive as no power,' while optimistic, symbolised the driving force behind his commitment to affordable electricity, which remained a focal point of his later life.

Bhabha's involvement extended beyond conferences. In February 1960, when Soviet leaders Nikita Khrushchev and Nikolai Bulganin visited India, Bhabha conducted a tour of TIFR for them. Later, in the summer of that year, Bhabha led an Indian delegation to the USSR. Subsequently, in February 1961, Bhabha announced that the USSR had agreed to construct a reactor for India. He publicly criticised the IAEA inspections required for reactors coming from the US, viewing them as an intrusion on Indian sovereignty. The USSR, not being an IAEA member, welcomed India's and other non-aligned nations' opposition to IAEA controls over their nuclear programmes. Despite an Indo-Soviet agreement signed on 7 October 1961, substantial progress resulting from this collaboration was limited.

❑

Last Days of Nehru and His Policy on Atomic Bombs with Bhabha

Bhabha and Nehru were resolute in safeguarding India's sovereignty in atomic matters from international oversight, while advocating strongly for international peace to mitigate the risks of an uncontrolled nuclear arms race. Their concerns about nuclear weapons extended beyond moral apprehensions, encompassing pragmatic considerations. Nehru's push for nuclear disarmament, articulated to both the US and the USSR, positioned India as a genuinely non-aligned state and significantly elevated its stature among developing nations. This stance accorded India a more substantial role in global diplomacy than its actual material power might have warranted.

Nehru's disarmament diplomacy was founded on the principle that international bodies like the United Nations Disarmament Commission should be inclusive, ensuring participation from non-nuclear weapon states. India advocated multilateralism in disarmament negotiations as a fundamental tenet of its policy. Even as India sought greater representation, it held that the primary responsibility for nuclear disarmament rested with the two major power blocs. India believed that radical solutions to disarmament were impractical, given that nuclear weapons had already become an integral part of the security policies of nuclear weapon states.

The Soviet nuclear test in 1949 and the hydrogen bomb testing in 1952 contributed to a heightened arms race. In April 1954, Nehru proposed a standstill agreement, which, although largely overlooked by the superpowers, significantly bolstered India's diplomatic standing in the UN and among third-world countries. It also firmly placed the necessity for a nuclear test ban on the global disarmament agenda. In 1958, the USSR declared a unilateral moratorium, and the Limited Test Ban Treaty, the first global disarmament treaty, took effect in 1963. Nehru was not only the initiator of this concept but also its most prominent public figure—he personified and articulated its significance, essence, and message.

India's early engagement in nuclear disarmament occurred at a time when it had no direct stake in nuclear disarmament discussions, given its status as a non-nuclear weapons state. However, this diplomatic positioning provided India with a pretext to refrain from participating in any arms control initiatives. In subsequent years, the disarmament agenda became a guise for India to practice realism while outwardly advocating idealism. This strategic approach allowed India to preserve its future options in the nuclear realm. Despite having made progress in nuclear capabilities, India was not yet a nuclear-armed state.

Nehru, the then Prime Minister of India, recognised the importance of atomic energy not only for peaceful purposes like generating electricity but also for the country's defence. He believed that nuclear energy would be a primary national power in the future, acknowledging its significance for national security. By that time, nuclear weapons had evolved into symbols of national power, determining a nation's position in the global hierarchy.

Nehru's stance on nuclear matters was somewhat contradictory. While he championed a world free of nuclear weapons, his actions revealed a duality in his thinking. He portrayed an image of wanting to prevent future generations from the perils of nuclear warfare while being a prominent figure in the non-aligned movement and envisioning a role in ensuring global peace. Although Nehru publicly expressed that India would not manufacture nuclear weapons, behind the scenes, figures like Bhabha, involved in India's nuclear programme, faced restrictions on developing nuclear weapons.

Nehru's public statements often appeared unwavering, asserting that India would never utilise atomic energy for malevolent purposes, irrespective of the circumstances. However, these assurances were tinged with doubt, as Nehru himself admitted that one couldn't accurately predict the future. This dichotomy in Nehru's stance on nuclear issues led to a complex and sometimes confounding narrative surrounding India's nuclear ambitions.

The statements made by Nehru consistently emphasised India's lack of interest in developing atomic bombs, affirming the country's commitment to atomic energy for peaceful purposes. Nevertheless, his statements towards the latter part of 1955 exhibited a certain ambivalence and a realisation of the potential importance of having the option of a nuclear weapon for strategic purposes. This contrasted with his broader public image as a proponent of peace and international cooperation.

While Nehru maintained a stance as a peacemaker and internationalist, the principal figure in India's nuclear programme, Homi Bhabha, foresaw a time when India might need to create a nuclear bomb and was quietly preparing for such an eventuality.

Bhabha was discreetly advancing the necessary groundwork for nuclear weapons development, continually seeking out foreign scientists to impart knowledge on chain reactions and recruiting talented individuals to assist in these efforts.

Evidence points to Nehru's underlying duality in intent. In 1958, he sanctioned Project Phoenix, aimed at extracting bomb-grade plutonium from the CIRUS reactor. This reactor's primary function was to generate plutonium as a by-product, indicating a swift route toward nuclear weapons development. Bhabha's influence in negotiating safeguards for the reactor's spent fuel rods, which contained uranium, reflected his strategy of ensuring India's control over the plutonium without international interference. This included mastering the technology for creating uranium fuel rods of requisite quality, a task facilitated by Brahm Prakash's collaboration.

These initiatives illustrate a dichotomy between Nehru's public stance on non-engagement in nuclear weaponry and the concealed strategic steps taken by Bhabha and his team toward India's potential nuclear capabilities.

The juxtaposition between Nehru's public declarations and the private conversations held by key figures, particularly Homi Bhabha, reflected a dichotomy in their stances concerning the development of nuclear weapons. Nehru repeatedly stated India's disinterest in manufacturing atomic bombs, emphasising India's commitment to using nuclear science for peaceful purposes, despite acknowledging the country's technical capability to produce such weapons within a few years.

However, private discussions among individuals like Bhabha, as described by John Cockcroft and George Perkovich, presented a different perspective. There were indications that Bhabha had ambitions to develop nuclear weapons, despite his public advocacy for the peaceful uses of nuclear energy. His conversations, which veered towards the potential of developing bombs for a "Plowshare" programme, highlighted a contrasting motivation behind the facade of peaceful nuclear initiatives.

According to George Perkovich, Bhabha's primary objective appeared to be acquiring nuclear weapons capability under the guise of ostensibly peaceful programmes. Reports suggest that as early as December 1959, Bhabha implied India's progress toward developing a bomb independently, awaiting only a political directive, though the timeline for such a capability was not specified.

An encounter between Nehru, Bhabha, and Kenneth D. Nichols in 1960, further highlights the nuanced discussions. Nichols, an American military engineer with significant experience in the US nuclear establishment, managed to persuade Bhabha about the superiority of American light water reactors over British gas-cooled reactors.

These accounts shed light on the contrast between public affirmations of non-nuclear weapons ambitions and private discussions hinting at covert aspirations for developing nuclear armaments in India. The context highlights the intricate and conflicting narratives surrounding India's nuclear ambitions during that era.

The conversations between Nehru, Bhabha, and Nichols shed light on the nuanced and paradoxical stance adopted by Nehru regarding India's nuclear capabilities. The interactions reveal the complexity in Nehru's approach—his public declarations promoting nuclear disarmament and a world free of atomic bombs seemingly contradicted by more private, candid discussions with key figures like Bhabha and Nichols.

In a meeting with Nichols, Nehru displayed extraordinary candour by inquiring if Bhabha could develop a nuclear bomb. Bhabha's affirmative response, indicating the potential to build a bomb within a year, was met with surprising openness by Nehru. He cautioned Bhabha not to proceed without his authorisation, an instruction that was unexpected, especially coming from a leader known for advocating peace.

It's noted that Bhabha's claim of being able to develop a bomb within a year was not based on factual grounds. Even in the most optimistic scenarios, such a timeline for bomb development was not feasible before 1963, as George Perkovich mentioned.

Contradicting the widely held belief that Nehru explicitly forbade Bhabha from developing a nuclear weapon, some biographers and accounts suggest that Nehru was not entirely against India having nuclear capabilities. His position seemingly leaned more toward not openly rejecting the idea of nuclear weapons while publicly advocating a world free from atomic bombs. He authorised substantial plans for Bhabha to establish comprehensive nuclear infrastructure capable of both generating nuclear energy and potentially constructing bombs.

Further insights into Nehru's response to Bhabha, as recalled by Bertrand Goldschmidt, revealed Nehru's position, indicating that India always held the door ajar for nuclear armament if the situation demanded. This stance was aimed at showcasing India's capability to build a bomb if necessary, as per Bhabha's perspective.

These narratives collectively reveal a dual approach characterised by Nehru's nuanced stance—a public narrative advocating peace and nuclear disarmament, while tacitly permitting the establishment of substantial nuclear infrastructure and leaving the possibility of a nuclear weapon open, for India, in specific circumstances.

The reluctance of Nehru to accept international offers of assistance for the development of atomic power plants reflects his belief that such support was a ploy by nuclear powers to prevent emerging nations from achieving nuclear self-sufficiency. The refusal of Eisenhower's offer, exemplified by Nehru's statement to Bhabha, highlights the political nature of decisions surrounding nuclear technology, indicating that these decisions were not within the purview of nuclear scientists alone.

During the Kennedy administration, there were notable gestures made towards India regarding nuclear capabilities. President Kennedy offered assistance for India to conduct a nuclear test. Kennedy, recognising China's advancements in nuclear testing and the potential security threat it posed, believed that allowing India, a democratic nation, to test a nuclear device before China would be beneficial. The aim was to strengthen India's security in the face of China's nuclear developments. Kennedy, in his letter to Nehru, stressed the paramount importance of national security.

The offer made by Kennedy underlined the gravity of geopolitical concerns and the acknowledgement of the strategic implications that nuclear capabilities held, especially within the context of the Sino-Indian relationship and the broader dynamics of the region. This gesture further emphasises how the pursuit of nuclear technology was intertwined with global geopolitics and strategic considerations, beyond the realm of mere scientific and technical exploration.

The dynamics of Nehru's response to Kennedy's offer, as highlighted by Rasgotra, were influenced by a multiplicity of factors. Nehru, despite not outright dismissing the offer, appeared hesitant to accept US assistance, reflecting his dedication to maintaining India's non-aligned status and commitment to global disarmament. This aligns with Nehru's unwavering advocacy for global disarmament, culminating in his pivotal role in the signing of the Partial Test Ban Treaty in 1963, which prohibited atmospheric nuclear weapon testing.

The potential impact of accepting Kennedy's offer, suggested as a possible deterrent against the 1962 Chinese attack and the 1965 Indo-Pak conflict, remains a subject of speculation and historical conjecture. Nehru's reservations toward accepting foreign assistance, in this case, might have stemmed from his inclination to balance India's foreign policy and maintaining independence from the influence of major powers.

In parallel, the interactions between Bhabha and the USSR point to India's exploration of diverse partnerships to acquire nuclear capabilities. Bhabha's attempts to engage with the Soviet Union for power plant technology highlight India's diplomatic manoeuvres to acquire necessary nuclear infrastructure and leverage assistance from different sources, such as the US and Canada, while also pursuing independent development in nuclear energy. These actions encapsulate India's strategy in leveraging international relationships to further its nuclear agenda.

The pursuit of nuclear capabilities in India, spearheaded by Nehru and Bhabha, was underpinned by a dual aspiration: the perceived advancements in nuclear technology offered India a fast track to modernity and global recognition. Both leaders believed that mastering nuclear technology, primarily in civil applications but also potentially in military aspects, would elevate India's international status and bolster its self-esteem. Amid the zeitgeist of the era, technological development and economic growth were seen as crucial markers of a nation's progress and a means to achieve a respected position within the international community.

India's desire to become proficient in nuclear technology was driven not only by aspirations of competing with Western nations in high technology but also by the necessity for self-reliance and indigenous development. The failure of civilian nuclear power production, which was envisaged as a solution for India's economic progress, led scientists to emphasise the military dimensions of nuclear technology. This shift highlighted the significance of nuclear weapons in projecting India as a major global power. Consequently, the emphasis moved away from nuclear technology's developmental potential, such as cheap electricity generation, towards the strategic aspects of nuclear weapons and the intangible notion of nuclear prestige associated with them.

The decision to collaborate with Canada for the CIRUS reactor in the mid-1950s was primarily geared towards quickly acquiring plutonium. Plutonium, generated as a by-product in the CIRUS reactor, was crucial for India's potential development of nuclear weapons. With no country willing to provide enriched uranium or plutonium without stringent safeguards, CIRUS provided India with a shortcut towards acquiring the materials necessary for nuclear weapons. Bhabha's opposition to safeguards at the Geneva conference was indicative of India's intention to keep the possibility of developing nuclear weapons open right from the outset of its nuclear programme.

In the early days of India's foray into nuclear technology, the inner workings and motivations of Homi Bhabha, the driving force behind the atomic energy establishment, were scarcely scrutinised by individuals outside this specialised field. Bhabha, wielding significant influence in these matters, exhibited a selective approach regarding safeguards associated with nuclear projects. Notably, he accepted and endorsed safeguards for specific reactors like those at Tarapur (TAPS I and II) and Rawatbhata (RAPS I and II), a decision seemingly dictated by circumstances.

Amid these pivotal moments, one of the critical junctures occurred in 1960 when the CIRUS reactor was poised to go critical. Bhabha, employing his persuasive skills, successfully conveyed to Prime Minister Nehru the necessity of establishing a reprocessing plant dedicated to extracting plutonium from the spent fuel rods of the reactor. This pivotal discussion led to Nehru's clearance for Project Phoenix in July 1958. This project aimed to process a substantial amount of fuel, targeting the recovery of 10 kg of plutonium from 20 tonnes of fuel every year. Such initiatives underlined India's strategic interest in accessing and processing critical nuclear materials, particularly plutonium, an essential element in potential nuclear weapon development.

France played a significant role in contributing to India's nuclear knowledge base. In 1960, the relocation of the Fontenay Aux Roses laboratories to Saclay prompted the French to offer an educational opportunity for Indian scientists to observe large-scale nuclear plant construction. Bhabha seized this opportunity to further India's nuclear capabilities by sending V.K. Iya, a scientist deeply involved in India's atomic pursuits, to gather intelligence regarding the manufacture of polonium, an element crucial to the triggering mechanism of atomic bombs. Iya, chosen by Bhabha in Paris and deputed to Saclay in 1955, learned extensively about polonium manufacturing and radioisotope production. This knowledge aided in his leadership in the chemistry division of the Atomic Energy Establishment and proved invaluable in subsequent crucial endeavours, notably in the preparation for the Pokhran explosion in 1974.

The increasing urgency in India's atomic endeavours became more apparent in 1961 when Nehru, alarmed by reports of China's advancements in nuclear testing, urged Bhabha to accelerate India's capabilities for a peaceful nuclear explosion. Despite Nehru's staunch stance against the development of nuclear weapons, he recognised the significance of a position of strength when advocating for a nuclear-free world. This strategic positioning was Bhabha's realm, as he began assembling a group of physicists led by RK Asundi. This team was discreetly assigned the task of investigating the physics underpinning nuclear explosions, focusing particularly on high-pressure physics and the compression dynamics of a plutonium sphere transitioning from a controlled reaction to an explosive mode. Members of this group, including G Murthy, were unaware of the broader context, interpreting the work as a purely theoretical exercise.

These series of key developments underlined the deliberate strides India was taking towards bolstering its nuclear capabilities, propelled by the strategic foresight of Bhabha and the supportive directives of Prime Minister Nehru, aligning with their vision of India as a prominent, technologically advanced nation in the global arena.

Bhabha's discretion and insistence on confidentiality within the group of physicists studying nuclear explosions were paramount. To ensure the utmost secrecy, MGK Menon issued a circular instructing the group to maintain strict confidentiality about their work. They were even assigned a designated room at the Tata Institute of Fundamental Research (TIFR), where they conducted their meetings and submitted their research papers directly to Bhabha. Bhabha's ire was evident when he discovered that the technicians at the CIRUS reactor were openly displaying the temperature required for heating the rods to produce weapons-grade plutonium. Realising the gravity of this highly sensitive information being exposed, which could be deciphered by a knowledgeable observer, he promptly ordered the removal of the display.

The trajectory towards India's nuclear weapon capability, particularly the clandestine aspect, gained momentum in 1962 with the amendment of the Atomic Energy Act. This revision significantly tightened the existing protocols of secrecy and augmented the AEC control over all atomic energy-related activities. Remarkably, the debates and discussions around the Bill, at the time of its enactment, didn't substantially focus on the traditionally emphasised 'peaceful uses' of atomic energy. Instead, there was a discernible undercurrent that silently associated nuclear power with potential military ends.

Nehru's apparent urgency in passing the Act was notable. Efforts were made to limit discussions and hasten the Bill's approval, with a sudden last minute alteration in the debate schedule. Moreover, a strict time limit of three hours was imposed for deliberations on the matter. The Act itself purported to facilitate the 'development, control, and use of atomic energy for the welfare of the people of India and other peaceful purposes, and for matters connected therewith'. The rather vague phrase 'matters connected therewith' left considerable room for interpretation, potentially encompassing India's subsequent pursuit of nuclear weapons. In essence, the 1962 Act served as the legal and institutional framework that enabled India's strategy of maintaining an open-ended nuclear option, shrouded in ambiguity.

Following the disastrous conflict with China in October 1962, which resulted in a humiliating defeat for Indian forces and left Prime Minister Nehru in a state of desolation, Bhabha perceived that India would face a prolonged period before achieving any form of parity with China in conventional warfare. This realisation motivated him to leverage the defeat against China as a means to advocate for India's nuclear weapons programme. About a month after the conflict, Bhabha penned a classified missive to Nehru outlining China's imminent nuclear testing and suggesting the path forward for India. Bhabha emphasised the urgency of prioritising the weapons programme and proposed that India should aim for a more significant nuclear programme than China's. He expressed the idea that India's capability to acquire a substantial quantity of plutonium within 18 months would serve as a deliberate demonstration that India had the technological capability to construct atomic weapons but had consciously chosen not to pursue this path.

In a subsequent meeting between Bhabha and Nehru, the exact details remain undisclosed. However, Bhabha, sharing insights with Rasgotra, conveyed certain aspects of the encounter. Bhabha mentioned his efforts to persuade Nehru to conduct a nuclear test but expressed that Nehru had vehemently opposed the idea. Nevertheless, Nehru instructed Bhabha to expedite the necessary steps leading to a peaceful nuclear explosion. Yet, Bhabha's aspirations were met with considerable setbacks during these discussions. The CIRUS reactor was experiencing erratic functionality, and the reprocessing plant, which Bhabha considered vital, encountered technological obstacles, delaying its commissioning.

Amid this period, when China's invasion had brought significant upheaval, JRD Tata extended an offer of assistance to India. This offer was later taken up by the newly appointed Defence Minister, YB Chavan, following VK Krishna Menon's dismissal due to his mishandling of the war and the subsequent public outcry. Chavan requested JRD Tata for a confidential report on India's future aviation necessities. The Tata report, titled 'Aircraft and Ancillary Electronic Equipment Required by the Defence Services,' was a collective effort involving Tata, the defence secretary, the foreign secretary, the three service chiefs, and Bhabha. It provided comprehensive recommendations concerning the required equipment and the expansion plans for the Indian Air Force over the following decade.

In July 1963, a noteworthy exchange occurred between Prime Minister Jawaharlal Nehru and the eminent nuclear physicist Homi Bhabha. Nehru had forwarded a passage from Edgar Snow's book, "The Other Side of the River," a text that offered insights into the Chinese Communist movement, particularly related to China's growing nuclear ambitions. Snow's perspective shed light on the potential psychological and political repercussions of China testing a nuclear device, prompting Bhabha to contemplate the measures India should take to counter such an eventuality.

Responding to Nehru's communication, Bhabha emphasised the urgency of India showcasing its potential to match China's nuclear capabilities if such a test were conducted by its neighbour. His response underscored the strategic imperative for India to prove its own nuclear capability in a brief time frame following China's test. Bhabha proposed that India should swiftly sign the Test Ban Treaty to signal its intention not to build atomic weaponry, but with a conditional clause. This stipulation aimed to reserve India's right to reconsider its commitment in the event of a neighbouring nation conducting a nuclear test. He envisioned a scenario where the balance of power in Asia would shift significantly in favour of China if India failed to attain nuclear capability.

However, the situation underwent a significant change as Nehru passed away on 27 May 1964, and Lal Bahadur Shastri succeeded him as the Prime Minister two weeks later. Bhabha expressed deep reverence for Nehru in an article composed after Nehru's demise, acknowledging the privilege of working alongside such an extraordinary leader for an extensive period.

The account highlighted Nehru's managerial approach, which emphasised delegating responsibilities and providing directives on policy matters while maintaining a keen interest in the department's progress without interfering in its day-to-day operations. Bhabha's tribute to Nehru's vision underscored the commitment to self-reliance in industrialisation and technological advancement, mirroring the essence of Nehru's ambition to establish a robust indigenous manufacturing capability without external reliance.

Additionally, the Science Advisory Committee, chaired by Bhabha, lauded Nehru's profound quest for knowledge, his inquisitive mindset, and his unwavering willingness to learn and teach, which paralleled the traits of a true man of science. Nehru reciprocated this admiration by acknowledging Bhabha's immense achievements and collaborative efforts within various spheres, particularly in the domain of atomic energy.

The commemorative occasion following Nehru's passing became a reflection not only on his leadership but also on his collaborative engagement with scientific and technological luminaries like Bhabha, emphasising a unified pursuit of progress and indigenous growth in India's scientific and industrial landscapes.

❏

Bhabha and His Nuclear Mission After Nehru

Lal Bahadur Shastri, who succeeded Nehru, held a Gandhian ideology starkly contrasting the urbane sophistication of Homi Bhabha, the eminent atomic authority. Known for his moral opposition to the bomb, Shastri also stood apart from the polished demeanour and leveraged his friendship with Nehru to navigate various issues. Hailing from modest origins, Shastri's humble demeanour contrasted with the suave social circles. Bhabha, accustomed to his direct access to the Prime Minister's office, felt the shift keenly, finding himself now needing a formal appointment to meet Shastri. Their communication faced challenges as Shastri found it challenging to grasp Bhabha's insights, adding to the latter's frustrations.

The dynamics changed with China's detonation of a nuclear device on 16 October 1964, breaching the Partial Test Ban Treaty, a significant moment marking India's first direct encounter with a nuclear threat. This event was unprecedented in independent India's history, particularly unsettling as the nation faced a hostile neighbour with newfound nuclear capabilities, especially after the recent loss in a war where China had seized extensive territories along the Himalayan frontier. Beyond the threat to India's territorial integrity, the country's international reputation hung in the balance.

China's nuclear test superseded India's regional and global leadership aspirations, especially following Nehru's death, leaving a vacuum in both leadership and international influence. The Chinese nuclear test thrust the issue of nuclear armament to the forefront of India's security policy, fundamentally reshaping the nation's approach to nuclear disarmament and arms control. National security took centre stage, altering India's diplomatic and strategic landscape in confronting the challenges of the nuclear age.

Following Nehru's passing, Homi Bhabha encountered hurdles in effectively communicating his perspectives to Lal Bahadur Shastri and other political figures. The Lyndon B. Johnson Library in Austin, Texas houses files detailing Indira Gandhi's inaugural visit to Washington as the Prime Minister in 1966. These archives contain confidential telegrams from the US embassy in Delhi, along with briefings prepared for President Lyndon B. Johnson by his advisers. A top-secret document dated December 1964 chronicles Bhabha's conversation with Spurgeon Keeney, the scientific adviser to the US president. It reports that during a comprehensive presentation to the Indian cabinet immediately after China's inaugural nuclear test, Bhabha had a revelation—most ministers seemed to struggle to grasp the technical details he was discussing.

Just eight days following the Chinese nuclear explosion, Bhabha seized the airwaves with a significant address on nuclear disarmament on United Nations Day, broadcasted over All India Radio. In his speech, Bhabha delved into the concept of nuclear deterrence, stressing that atomic weaponry endowed a state with the capability to deter an attack from a significantly more potent adversary. He emphasised that the significance of nuclear weapons lay in deterring a state with such armaments from utilising them offensively. A key aspect of his speech, however, was his claim that constructing a two-megaton nuclear bomb was not financially burdensome. Bhabha estimated that a 10-kiloton explosion would cost 17.5 lakh, while a 2-megaton explosion would be around 30 lakh. He asserted that atomic explosives were considerably cheaper than conventional explosives. To illustrate, he remarked that maintaining a stockpile of about 50 atomic bombs would cost less than 10 crores, and a similar quantity of 50-tonne bombs would amount to around 15 crores. These expenses, Bhabha suggested, were negligible compared to the military budgets of numerous countries. He urged the United Nations to foster an environment supportive of nations possessing the capability to produce atomic weapons yet choosing not to do so voluntarily.

Bhabha's attempts to articulate the nuances of nuclear technology to the political elite were challenging. His efforts to portray the cost-effectiveness of nuclear armaments and advocate for an atmosphere conducive to countries refraining from nuclear weaponization revealed the complexity of disseminating his views within the political corridors of India.

Bhabha's claim regarding the cost of nuclear weapons was rooted in calculations published in a paper by the Lawrence Radiation Laboratory in Livermore, United States. He vigorously advocated for the government to reach a decision on nuclear weapon development. During that period, the reprocessing plant in Trombay had commenced operations, providing India with the capacity to extract plutonium, a key element in crafting nuclear armaments. Even before the Chinese nuclear test, Bhabha publicly announced in London on 4 October 1964, that India could conduct an atomic bomb test within 18 months if such a directive was issued. In a bold challenge directed at Lal Bahadur Shastri, he remarked, "But I do not think such a decision will be taken."

Shastri, who was attending a meeting of non-aligned nations in Cairo at the time, maintained that India's nuclear establishment was strictly instructed to avoid any experimentation or development of devices not essential for the peaceful utilisation of nuclear energy.

The Prime Minister was hesitant to approve a nuclear weapons programme as it would signify a significant deviation from India's longstanding stance. Bhabha's vocal support for the bomb did not align with Shastri's perspective. Moreover, Shastri, in his capacity as the Prime Minister, was acutely aware of the nation's precarious economic condition. Following the 1962 conflict, the expenses associated with conventional defence had surged. Internally, India was grappling with an unprecedented food crisis.

Toward the end of October 1964, two press commentaries shed light on the ongoing debate about India's nuclear ambitions. The discussion surrounding the nuclear question was multifaceted, blending issues of economic strain, national security, and the contrast between Bhabha's advocacy for nuclear development and Shastri's cautious approach.

In a significant turn of events, in October 1964, the media became a focal point for the national discussion about India's nuclear prospects. Inder Malhotra, contributing to The Statesman, ignited a lively debate with his assertion that forgoing the development of a nuclear bomb was an unsustainable decision. He emphasised Bhabha's estimates on the cost of nuclear weapons, underscoring the notion that these arms weren't entirely cost-prohibitive. Malhotra's perspective raised the argument that the only true deterrent against a nuclear bomb was another nuclear bomb, effectively shifting the discourse. This viewpoint prompted a re-evaluation of India's strategic decisions, aligning with Bhabha's premise.

Simultaneously, an article published in the Hindustan Times, seemingly influenced by Bhabha's outlook, proudly enumerated the remarkable accomplishments of the Atomic Energy Establishment of Trombay (AEET). The piece boldly indicated that Indian scientists had taken China's nuclear explosion in their stride, expressing confidence rooted in the belief that India could have developed a nuclear bomb 18 months before China's test. The unchallenged nature of this claim bolstered the perception that India held the potential for nuclear weapon development long before the Chinese detonation, heightening the nation's stance in this pivotal discussion.

Contrary to these assertions, Romesh Thapar, contributing to the Economic and Political Weekly, presented a dissenting view. He questioned Bhabha's cost assessments for nuclear weapons, highlighting the potential for escalating expenses once the programme was in motion. This critical evaluation of Bhabha's claims marked a courageous departure from the prevalent discourse. Thapar expressed scepticism about the transformative capability of a bomb held by a nation with limited resources when numerous other countries possessed greater quantities of nuclear weapons and the means to deliver them strategically. This divergent viewpoint challenged the prevailing narrative about India's nuclear aspirations, stirring a dialogue on the risks, costs, and efficacy of pursuing a nuclear weapons programme.

Bhabha's public address on nuclear disarmament applied immense pressure on Shastri to consider authorising a distinct nuclear weapons programme. The Indian National Congress (INC), Shastri's party, was not exempt from the agitation concerning the nuclear issue. Advocates for the bomb capitalised on Bhabha's speech, utilising it as evidence that nuclear armament could be effortlessly manufactured at a reasonably low cost, even by a resource-strapped nation like India. The political storm catalysed further discussions about India's nuclear path within the INC.

During a crucial Congress Committee meeting held from 7th to 9th November 1964, Shastri disputed Bhabha's estimates regarding the cost of a bomb. He expressed his own calculations, indicating that producing a single bomb would incur a significantly higher expenditure than Bhabha's estimate. Shastri asserted that the creation of one bomb would cost between 40 to 50 crores, a significant contrast to Bhabha's projection of 10 crores for 50 atom bombs. He further emphasised that the responsibility to safeguard the nation rested with the government and called for appropriate defensive measures. Shastri's stand, supported by VK Krishna Menon and other INC leaders, gained ascendancy, showcasing a shift in power dynamics and a clear delineation of authority.

Notably, Bhabha's relationship with Krishna Menon was not amicable. An anecdote following India's first nuclear test at Pokhran in May 1974 revealed Krishna Menon's dissatisfaction. While ailing and having just a few months to live, Krishna Menon summoned Indira Gandhi and expressed his disapproval. This event marked a moment of tension and contention, highlighting the complex interactions between prominent figures in India's nuclear history.

Initially, Bhabha had reservations about PN Haksar, India's ambassador to Austria in the 1960s. As Vienna served as the IAEA headquarters, Haksar, in his diplomatic capacity, represented India on its board. Bhabha was initially wary of Haksar due to his allegiance to Krishna Menon. Nevertheless, Haksar's appointment as a member with full authority to articulate India's stance on nuclear non-proliferation and the imperative for atomic energy in the country swiftly transformed Bhabha's perceptions. This transition underscored the shifting dynamics and alignments within India's nuclear policy landscape.

Following the critical reception of his UN day speech by Shastri and Krishna Menon, Bhabha attempted to rectify the misperception about his stance on nuclear weapons in an interview with The Times of India on 17 November 1964. Bhabha clarified that his cost estimates were based on American figures for Peaceful Nuclear Explosions (PNEs). He emphasised the considerable achievements of the Atomic Energy Establishment of Trombay (AEET) and reiterated that the fundamental issue was not India's inability to create nuclear weapons or the financial incapacity to develop them but the political decision to refrain from their production. Shastri, wary of Bhabha's estimates, even sought a cost assessment of the bomb from the Harold Wilson government in the UK, in case India were to pursue its development. The report that ensued estimated a cost of about $350 million for creating the bomb, with an ongoing expense of $50 million. These costs, however, were deemed significantly inflated and were not officially communicated to the Indian government.

The subsequent discussions in the Lok Sabha in November 1964 revealed varied opinions regarding Bhabha's cost estimations and his perceived advocacy for a nuclear bomb. Krishna Menon, among others, challenged Bhabha's cost calculations and the appropriateness of his seeming advocacy for the bomb. On the other hand, some politicians who supported the bomb rallied behind Bhabha, using the figures he presented in his speech as a defence. Bhabha's statements were particularly well received by certain politicians, primarily from the Jan Sangh, who had long been proponents of an Indian nuclear bomb. Subsequently, on 27 November, Hukum Chand Kachwai, a Jan Sangh Member of Parliament from Dewas, introduced a motion in the Lok Sabha calling for the production of nuclear weapons. The debate unfolded amid strong and opposing perspectives on the nuclear issue within the Indian political landscape.

Following the discussion in the Lok Sabha, Shastri rebutted the bomb lobby's interpretation of Bhabha's intentions, clarifying that the production costs mentioned by Bhabha referred to those in the United States, and if produced in India, the costs would remain prohibitively high. Moreover, Shastri emphasised that manufacturing such weapons would deviate from the Gandhian principles India held dear and posed a threat not just to the country but to humanity at large. Although Shastri faced defensive challenges during the debate, a majority from the INC ensured that the resolution calling for the manufacture of nuclear weapons was defeated.

While Shastri secured victory against the resolution through a voice vote, his speech contained subtle yet significant concessions, which went relatively unnoticed at the time. He mentioned that India's nuclear establishments would continue their dedication to peaceful activities, which would now include the preparation of Peaceful Nuclear Explosions (PNES) for purposes like tunnelling through mountains. Shastri underlined that Bhabha had made it clear to him that such technologies could be harnessed for peaceful benefits and national development. A substantial part of Shastri's speech referred to Bhabha, explaining that Bhabha's intentions had been misconstrued as advocating for a nuclear bomb. Instead, Shastri underscored that Bhabha supported utilising atomic energy for peaceful uses, such as facilitating the excavation of mountainous terrains. The exchange between Bhabha and Shastri influenced Shastri's perspectives and played a pivotal role in the nuanced discussions during the debate.

What is truly notable is that during that time, Shastri unintentionally initiated a potential pathway towards the development of nuclear weaponry. Whether Shastri was strategically searching for a political compromise or genuinely convinced that the pursuit of peaceful explosions was distinct from producing weapons remains uncertain. Shastri, a modest individual who concluded his formal education at 17 and had limited exposure to international travel before assuming the role of Prime Minister, possessed little to no expertise in nuclear physics or technology. The journalist who astutely comprehended the situation was Inder Malhotra, foreseeing a policy shift after China's nuclear test and recognising the significance of Shastri's address to Parliament regarding peaceful nuclear explosions. In a series of five articles for The Statesman, Malhotra outlined the concealed policy transformation.

RK Laxman, the renowned cartoonist, crafted a drawing that he presented to Jamshed Bhabha. The illustration portrayed Shastri as an angel with wings, holding leaves in his hands, while Bhabha placed a halo on his head, and below them were the words, 'Atom for Peace'. In an earlier cartoon by Laxman, Nehru was depicted driving a bullock cart of progress with atomic wheels in a model, and the common man appeared as a perplexed passenger. Even the expression on the face of the bull reflected amazement at the innovative wheels. Bhabha admired Laxman's cartoons and had one of them enlarged and displayed in his room. Additionally, a cartoon portraying Bhabha studying the atom was published in the October 1984 edition of Science Today.

In a note dated November 1964, KR Narayanan, the director of the China Division at the Ministry of External Affairs, outlined the altered political landscape of Asia and the world following the Chinese nuclear explosion. Narayanan advocated for India to produce an atom bomb, emphasising that possessing such a weapon would enable the country to significantly influence the disarmament arena. He drew parallels with the historical figure Ashoka, suggesting that only when India possessed the bomb could it renounce it in a compelling and impactful manner, resembling Ashoka's renunciation.

The Indian nuclear policy had seemingly aligned with Bhabha's aspirations, which aimed at the development of explosives for peaceful purposes. Bhabha recognised that an overt bomb-building programme could provoke punitive reactions from countries like the US and Canada. However, a move towards the development of peaceful nuclear explosives was perceived as less likely to attract recriminations, particularly considering that the US itself had a programme focused on peaceful nuclear explosives called Project Plowshare. The USSR similarly claimed they had used such explosives for developmental projects. Consequently, Shastri's statement in India did not raise considerable concerns. Nevertheless, experts noted that a peaceful nuclear explosion could underscore India's capability to create a bomb.

Shastri's initial stance against the bomb had not been well received within his own party. However, by allowing peaceful explosions, Shastri strengthened his position. This decision did not disturb India's nuclear collaborations with the US and Canada, and it managed to bring Bhabha onto Shastri's side. Raja Ramanna highlighted that the idea of peaceful explosions possibly originated from Bhabha himself. Bhabha's team of scientists shared a profound commitment to expediting the nuclear bomb's development to elevate India's status.

Khera, the cabinet secretary from 1962 to 1964, noted Homi Bhabha's strong inclination to prepare comprehensively for the creation of a nuclear bomb. Those familiar with Bhabha's work and those who collaborated with him were keenly aware of his fervent dedication to having all the necessary components in place for the bomb.

Given the potential extended timeline for India to develop a credible deterrent, Shastri sought diplomatic solutions to counter the looming Chinese threat. During a state visit to London in December 1964, he raised this issue with British Prime Minister Harold Wilson. However, Shastri's attempts were met with disapproval in the Indian press, which criticised his pursuit of a nuclear shield, deeming it as contradictory to India's non-aligned stance. In a press conference, Shastri clarified that he was not only seeking protection for India but for all non-nuclear nations, suggesting that major nuclear powers should discuss measures to sustain global peace.

Meanwhile, back in India, pressure mounted on Bhabha to live up to his earlier assertion of creating a bomb within 18 months. Homi Sethna and Raja Ramanna expressed doubts about achieving this goal. Sethna speculated that they might assemble an explosive device but were likely unable to produce a portable bomb.

Ramanna was more sceptical, believing it was an unattainable goal. He believed that Bhabha's statement was a result of immense pressure to deliver on his claim. Ramanna's pragmatic view partly stemmed from the challenges faced by Project Phoenix, established to reprocess spent fuel from CIRUS and extract plutonium. Although they commenced reprocessing plutonium in mid-1964, the plant experienced irregular operation. Shastri inaugurated the plant on 22 January 1965, underscoring its relevance to India's peaceful nuclear explosion programme. Bhabha intended to signal to China that India possessed weapons-grade plutonium and had the capability to create a bomb if needed. Shastri even proposed, somewhat naively, that other nations could utilise India's facility for plutonium reprocessing.

Bhabha's audacious endeavour was quite evidently his own brainchild, an initiative that didn't stem from any request by Bhabha himself for such an assertion. His fervour for making their intentions known was reflected even in the vivid visual transformation of the reprocessing plant. Choosing to paint the funnel of the otherwise dull grey reprocessing plant in a striking shade of bright red, Bhabha conveyed to Ramanna, "Let the world take heed; we are fully prepared."

Despite Shastri's attempts to secure a nuclear defence for India, he encountered a setback as Bhabha conveyed the uncooperative stance of the United States. Faced with the stark reality that the Atomic Energy Establishment of Trombay (AEET) could not possibly develop a nuclear explosive within the lofty 18-month deadline, Bhabha discreetly sought assistance from the US around late 1964 or early 1965. By early 1965, Bhabha, pragmatic in his approach, had reassessed the timeline for the bomb's development, scaling it back to a more practical five-year timeframe. In the INC's annual conference in January 1965, there were strong arguments presented in favour of acquiring nuclear armament, stirred by the memories of India's struggle with China. Alternatively, some delegates suggested India should seek security under the protective umbrella of either the US or USSR. Despite the prevailing push for nuclear armament, Shastri, a firm opponent of nuclear weapons on moral grounds, advocated adhering to the no-bomb policy. He successfully steered a resolution through, asserting that, for the time being, India would confine its nuclear endeavours strictly to peaceful objectives. Shastri's emphasis on accelerating the advancement of nuclear energy for peaceful purposes assuaged opposition within his party and earned the support of the press.

During his discussions with US officials at the State Department in February 1965, Bhabha underlined the urgency for India to accomplish a significant peaceful feat to counterbalance the prestige China had gained among Africans and Asians. Highlighting the capabilities of the plutonium reprocessing plant, Bhabha conveyed India's potential, stating it was substantial enough to process all the plutonium from the reactors they were constructing, signifying that within five years, India could potentially manufacture a hundred nuclear bombs annually. Consequently, the Times, in its tribute to Bhabha, underscored India's latent capability for nuclear armament, emphasising the Indian government's strategic preparedness for the possible production of plutonium bombs in the future.

A year following Bhabha's passing, the discussion during the memorial lecture held in his honour at the Royal Institution in London provided intriguing insights into Bhabha's stance on the proliferation of nuclear armaments in India. Cockcroft, while reminiscing about Bhabha, shed light on the contrast between Bhabha's public avowal to adhere to the Indian government's anti-nuclear weapons policy and his private sentiments expressed in more intimate settings. Cockcroft suggested that in discreet, limited forums, Bhabha seemed to lean towards supporting the construction of plutonium-based bombs for civil engineering applications, an initiative known as the Plowshare programme. This proposal aimed to utilise such bombs for the creation of storage cavities, harbours, or canals as part of various civil engineering projects.

During the same Royal Institution gathering, MGK Menon argued that India's intention behind establishing the reprocessing plant predated the 1962 Sino-Indian conflict, emphasising its primary purpose for the reprocessing of fuel rods, not for the manufacturing of nuclear weapons. However, Menon's explanation, aiming to serve as a justification, appeared to hold minimal sway. The prevalent distrust between India and China was a well-established fact, dating back to China's occupation of Tibet in 1950. Border tensions between the two nations were prevalent even before the 1962 conflict. Notably, prior to the war in October 1962, India had already taken cognizance of China's advancements in their nuclear weapons programmes, setting a context that substantiated India's concerns regarding its neighbour's military capabilities.

The declassified documents offer a revealing narrative, showcasing Bhabha's endeavour to engage with the United States regarding the Plowshare device or its blueprints during late 1964 and early 1965. This pursuit occurred without Bhabha's knowledge of the US AEC concurrent inclusion of Plowshare projects in its contemplation of potential cooperative areas with India. Bhabha himself persisted in pursuing the Plowshare matter, particularly when former presidential science adviser Jerome Wiesner visited Trombay on January 19, 1965.

During Wiesner's visit, he left a comprehensive report for US AEC member John Palfrey, who was scheduled to arrive in India for the inauguration of the reprocessing plant at Trombay.

A cable from the US State Department to Palfrey gave him the green light to discuss Plowshare-like initiatives with Bhabha. Wiesner's report highlighted a critical observation: Bhabha had significantly underestimated the expenses linked to producing a bomb and desired a more accurate cost estimation from the United States. In his report, Wiesner outlined Bhabha's desire for authorisation and resources to progress without an ultimate decision concerning an actual explosion. Notably, there was no comprehensive evaluation of the real cost or the strategic implications of deploying such a weapon system.

This series of events shed light on the significant flaw within the Indian nuclear programme. It revealed a lack of effective mechanisms for independent scrutiny of the claims and proposals put forward by the AEC, particularly Bhabha. The dearth of transparent processes and informed debate hindered India's nuclear policy formulation for an extensive period. As expert George Perkovich highlighted, the opacity and independence of the nuclear establishment, combined with the deficiency of qualified scientific expertise outside that closed circle, severely compromised the policy-making process. This lack of transparency restricted the ability of leaders like Nehru and Shastri, engaged in debates over nuclear policy, to adequately scrutinise Bhabha's assertions.

Bhabha's visit to Washington in late February 1965 provided an insight into the nuclear discussions he held with George Ball, the undersecretary of state. During these discussions, Bhabha expressed his perspective on the advancements of various nations in nuclear capabilities. He posited that China's swift progress in nuclear development might have been influenced by the USSR's blueprints for a nuclear device. In a rather direct appeal for American assistance, Bhabha indicated to Ball that with access to a US blueprint, India could produce a device in six months, whereas independently, this endeavour would require 18 months.

The US embassy's scientific attaché's report from this period shed light on the challenges confronted by India's reprocessing plant. The report highlighted the plant's heavy dependence on supplies from the US and other foreign sources, leading to intermittent shutdowns due to the unavailability of crucial components. Ultimately, the report concluded that supporting India with something substantial to elevate its status comparable to China's nuclear capabilities appeared to be a formidable challenge.

By April 1965, the US Atomic Energy Commission took a more conservative stance concerning nuclear cooperation with India. Bhabha and Glenn Seaborg, a key American scientist, met to discuss potential collaboration, but Seaborg emphasised limiting cooperation to educational lectures and assisting with engineering issues. Strict controls over technological transfers were sought by the Americans, driven by political considerations, and this precluded the provision of Plowshare device blueprints or plans to India at that time.

In a letter addressed to the chairman of the US Congress Joint Committee on Energy dated April 30, 1965, Seaborg outlined possible collaborative endeavours between India and the US. However, the letter conspicuously omitted any reference to cooperation on a Plowshare device. Additionally, it highlighted Bhabha's request for a moderate quantity of plutonium, which seemed peculiar considering the recent launch of the reprocessing plant at Trombay. This implied the plant was not functioning optimally. The absence of any mention of a Plowshare device implied that Bhabha's request was perceived to have undesirable implications for nuclear proliferation.

Bhabha's request to the United States not only brought into question his earlier claims about India's capability to develop a nuclear weapon within 18 months but also underscored the somewhat independent nature of his dealings in nuclear affairs, leaving doubts as to whether he had informed Shastri about his plea to the Americans. There is evidence suggesting that Shastri excluded Bhabha from certain high-level discussions on nuclear policy, indicating a certain degree of distancing between them.

Bhabha's appeal for assistance coincided with a time when the US was actively formulating its non-proliferation policy. As the Lyndon B. Johnson administration solidified its support for the non-proliferation treaty, the chances of India obtaining any technology from the US diminished. Ultimately, India did not receive any support from the United States and had to pursue its nuclear ambitions independently.

Upon receiving Shastri's approval for a project he had long championed, Bhabha acted swiftly. In April 1965, he established a small group called the Study of Nuclear Explosions for Peaceful Purposes (SNEPP) and placed Ramanna in charge. Ramanna recalls Bhabha's evident excitement as he proudly presented the document bearing Shastri's endorsement. Bhabha assembled a team of physicists to assist Ramanna and, in an attempt to keep the project discreet, advised him not to disclose the initiative to EC Allardice, housing the group in a separate building.

During a visit to Paris in the spring of 1965, Bhabha met with TS Murthy, a young scientist undergoing training at Saclay. He outlined the importance of mastering polonium extraction, a crucial component in the trigger mechanism for atomic bombs. Bhabha urged Murthy, who later played a significant role in the Pokhran explosion in 1974, to delve into the subject and absorb as much knowledge about polonium as possible.

By December 1965, Shastri directed Bhabha to accelerate plans for a Peaceful Nuclear Explosion (PNE), marking a pivotal moment in India's nuclear trajectory.

During the 1965 war, as per Sethna, a distressed Lal Bahadur Shastri sought options from Bhabha. In response, Bhabha mentioned the ongoing work on the Peaceful Nuclear Explosion (PNE). Shastri permitted the continuation of the project but emphasised that no experiments were to be conducted without explicit clearance from the Cabinet. Bhabha immediately summoned Sethna, instructing him to assemble the necessary groups essential for preparing the device. This included separate groups dedicated to engineering, measurements, and device production.

Tragically, Shastri passed away in Tashkent on 11 January 1966, shortly after signing the Tashkent Declaration. His successor, Indira Gandhi, assumed responsibility for nuclear affairs but encountered a significant setback as Bhabha was killed in an air crash on 24 January 1966. Given the classified nature of atomic matters, very few individuals were privy to the complete agenda. With both Shastri and Bhabha no longer alive, and no comprehensive recording of the discussions and reasoning behind pivotal decisions, there was a notable absence of authoritative figures in the know. Bhabha's untimely demise created a substantial void in India's nuclear policy formulation.

❑

Great Loss or
Great Conspiracy?

While overseeing atomic energy concerns, Bhabha was instrumental in expanding the Tata Institute of Fundamental Research (TIFR). By the late 1950s, TIFR had outgrown its premises at the Bombay Yacht Club. Bhabha began searching for a more expansive location and set his sights on an area named Colaba, situated at the tip of the Bombay island. This area was under the control of the Indian Navy, which had housed barracks for soldiers during World War II. When Bhabha requested a donation of land from this area, the defence ministry initially declined. Subsequently, he approached Nehru, despite uncertainties regarding a contradiction from Defence Minister V Krishna Menon, who was a close associate of Nehru. However, Nehru supported Bhabha's request, leading to the allocation of a piece of land to TIFR, albeit with certain restrictions imposed by the Navy.

Bhabha engaged architect Helmuth Bartsch to design new buildings for TIFR. Bartsch, a well-regarded architect influenced by Bauhaus style, integrated these ideas into the design of the new TIFR buildings. In 1962, Bartsch praised Bhabha's continuous encouragement and valuable suggestions that contributed to the development of the building, expressing hope that it would not only serve its function but also provide enjoyment (as stated in "A Masterful Spirit").

The construction of the TIFR complex, initiated by Nehru's foundation laying ceremony in 1954, spanned about eight years, culminating in its formal inauguration in 1962. The inauguration was attended by various international scientists, including TD Lee, the Nobel Prize-winning physicist from 1957.

As TIFR evolved into a mature institute, Bhabha introduced new research units, including one dedicated to molecular biology. Back in 1944, Sir AV Hill had corresponded with Bhabha about the necessity of biological research. At the time, Bhabha was hesitant about initiating this research area until he found a mature individual capable of independently establishing and leading a research group.

During a visit to Cambridge in 1962, Bhabha encountered Leo Szilard, a renowned physicist known for his role in the Manhattan Project. Szilard informed Bhabha about a young molecular biologist at the University of Pennsylvania, Obaid Siddiqi. Recalling the incident, Siddiqi mentioned that within a week of their conversation, he received a letter from Bhabha inviting him to join TIFR. Initially lacking a biology unit in 1961, Bhabha encouraged Siddiqi to acquire the necessary equipment, and subsequently, the molecular biology unit flourished. Siddiqi himself received the honour of being named a Fellow of the Royal Society (FRS).

The field of radio astronomy, although initiated by Karl Jansky's groundbreaking observations of radio signals from celestial sources beyond the solar system, didn't fully take shape until after World War II. In the 1950s, significant progress in radio astronomy was being made in the USA, UK, and Australia. Even in India, KS Krishnan envisioned establishing a radio astronomy group at the National Physical Laboratory in New Delhi. He was inspired by the extraordinary discoveries presented at the 1952 General Assembly of the International Radio Scientific Union in Sydney. Krishnan sent a young student, Govind Swarup, under a fellowship from the Colombo Plan to Sydney. The initial efforts to build a radio interferometer, aimed at amalgamating radio signals from an array to create a "radio image" of celestial bodies, were underway.

Bhabha, during his visit to the Potts Hill radio astronomical observatory in 1955, was captivated by the emergence of this new scientific field. This excitement led to several Indian students pursuing their PhDs in the USA and Australia, including Govind Swarup, T.K. Menon, Mukul Kundu, and T. Krishnan. W.N. Christiansen, a pioneer in radio interferometry, encouraged these young Indian radio astronomers to unite in their pursuit and overcome bureaucratic obstacles in India.

In 1961, the four Indian astronomers convened at a meeting of the International Astronomical Union in Berkeley and collectively decided to return to India to establish a radio astronomy group. They presented their plan to five scientific organisations in India. Bart Bok of Harvard University, a renowned astronomer, endorsed their return to India as a group, emphasising its rarity and the scientific significance for the nation's advancement. Bhabha, in a telegram to all four individuals in January 1962, confirmed the formation of a radio astronomy group and followed up with a detailed letter outlining the ambitious potential for their work in India.

This momentous decision marked Govind Swarup's joining of TIFR in 1963. During that year, while presenting a paper in Nature, Swarup identified a critical application of lunar occultation to test theories of the universe. However, this required a larger telescope, four times the size of existing radio telescopes. Swarup conceived the idea of constructing a massive cylindrical radio telescope set on a hill inclined to match the Earth's axis. When he discussed this idea with Bhabha, the latter displayed a keen interest, spending over two hours probing Swarup before responding with great enthusiasm. Bhabha advised Swarup against writing a project report immediately but emphasised the importance of assembling a capable team first. Bhabha suggested that once the team was in place, they could then proceed with the detailed project report and its subsequent design and construction.

The Ooty radio telescope had its inception in a test array constructed at Kalyan near Bombay, eventually finding a suitable hill near Ooty that aligned with the necessary requirements. Bhabha was eager to secure the land promptly, despite some officials questioning the urgency of the matter in contrast to the billions of years the stars endure. Following discussions with government officials after Nehru's passing, a 600-acre plot was allocated for TIFR's experiments, marking the genesis of the Ooty radio telescope. The installation of cosmic ray experimental equipment also occurred at this site, and the Ooty radio telescope was completed in 1970, continuing its operations to this day.

Bhabha also played a pivotal role in the establishment of Indian space research. After the launch of Sputnik by the Soviet Union in 1958, Bhabha advocated for the Department of Atomic Energy to take charge of space research. His efforts led to the inauguration of the first seminar on Space Physics in 1963. Bhabha emphasised the importance of proactive participation in space research to prevent India from lagging behind in technological advancements. His foresight regarding the significance of this field indeed turned out to be prophetic.

However, Bhabha did not witness India's ascension as a significant player in international space research. Following Bhabha's demise, Vikram Sarabhai carried forward the torch of space research. Initially, the Indian Space Research Organisation (ISRO) remained under the Department of Atomic Energy's control, with a distinct Ministry of Space established in 1972.

Bhabha was forward-thinking in recognising the criticality of computational facilities for scientific research. He emphasised the necessity of advancements in electronics research, which materialised through the electronics group at TIFR and AEET. Under his guidance, TIFR undertook the task of designing and constructing a large digital computer named TIFRAC, marking one of the country's initial forays into building computers.

Homi Bhabha's influence on the international scientific community continued to grow steadily. His remarkable contributions were acknowledged by prestigious bodies, such as the American Academy of Arts and Sciences, electing him as an honorary fellow in 1959. Further, in 1963, he received a rare honour for a scientist outside the USA by being elected a foreign associate of the National Academy of Sciences.

During the aftermath of the Sino-Indian conflict in 1962, Bhabha offered his expertise to help develop electronic systems for defence. He proposed the establishment of an Electronics Committee to assess the country's electronic needs and recommend strategies for its planned development, aiming for self-sufficiency in this field. Unfortunately, he passed away before the committee could present its report. Later, the Department of Electronics (DoE) was founded in 1970, although its headquarters were established in New Delhi, distinct from the DAE and the DoS.

The geopolitical scenario grew more complex post the Sino-Indian war, particularly after China's nuclear testing in 1964. Bhabha, in a public broadcast on All India Radio in October 1964, suggested that India could produce a nuclear bomb within eighteen months if the need arose, using the accumulated plutonium from Indian reactors. Despite the Indian government's declared policy against developing nuclear weapons, Bhabha's private discussions with associates indicated an ambivalent attitude. After China's nuclear test, he expressed the desire for India to be capable of creating plutonium bombs if the government chose to do so.

Tragically, Bhabha's life was cut short by a devastating event. While en route to attend a meeting in Vienna on 24 January 1966, the Air India flight 101, named 'Kanchenjunga,' met with a fatal accident, crashing on Mont Blanc in the Alps near the Franco-Italian border. The crash resulted in the loss of all 117 passengers, including Bhabha. The investigation concluded that severe weather conditions and miscommunication between the air traffic controller in Geneva and the pilot led to the crash. Nevertheless, conspiracy theories surrounding sabotage, particularly after Bhabha's statement about a potential Indian atomic bomb, have persisted. Though parts of the wreckage were found by climbers since 2008, no direct evidence of foul play has been discovered thus far.

Bhabha's untimely and accidental demise struck India at a time when it was already reeling from the loss of Lal Bahadur Shastri in Tashkent, a mere two weeks before the tragedy. Following these events, Indira Gandhi took the reins as India's new Prime Minister, while Vikram Sarabhai assumed leadership at the Department of Atomic Energy.

However, Bhabha's enduring legacy remains palpable in many aspects of modern-day India. The Tata Institute of Fundamental Research (TIFR) stands as a preeminent scientific institution in the country, and the Bhabha Atomic Research Centre (BARC) continues to strive towards the fulfilment of India's three-stage nuclear power programme. Although discussions might arise about the appropriateness of some of Bhabha's visionary plans, his achievements need to be contextualised within the period he lived in and the individuals he collaborated with. Hindsight criticism is easy, but considering the tremendous impact Bhabha had on India within a short span, it's undeniably remarkable. His inspirational leadership in organising scientific research, his zeal to leave an indelible mark not just for himself but for a nation to be proud of, continues to motivate young science students in India.

A visit to the radio astronomy centre, cosmic ray detectors in Ooty, or the newly constructed gamma ray telescope in Hanle, Ladakh – designed by BARC scientists, peering into the vast universe – evokes the realisation that all these ventures originated from one man's dream.

The first day cover of the postage stamp issued in Bhabha's honour by the Indian government encapsulated his essence. It depicted him contemplatively overlooking Trombay, where he established his nuclear city, an artist's palette beside him, and beneath him, the 'Ode to Joy' theme from Beethoven's Ninth Symphony.

He could be considered one of the last Renaissance men the world has known. Bhabha was driven by an inner aesthetic that encompassed a spectrum of visions, from mathematical theories of particles to architectural designs for his institutions, fostering an atmosphere of scientific exploration in India that he envisioned. He once expressed, 'Art, music, poetry, and everything else that I do have this one purpose—increasing the intensity of my consciousness and life.' His achievements within the short span of his life are a testament to this credo.

In 2017, Daniel Roche, a Swiss climber with a passion for aviation, made a startling discovery in the Alps: the remnants of an aircraft that could potentially be linked to one of two Air India crashes. Among the debris, Roche found scattered limbs and a jet engine at the crash site, prompting his belief that this wreckage may be associated with Air India flight 101. Roche's theory posited that Flight 101 might have encountered another aircraft, resulting in a collision that led to the crash. He explained that due to the high-altitude conditions with minimal oxygen, there had been insufficient combustion to generate an explosion post-impact.

The discovery triggered speculation and resurrected theories around the mysterious Air India crash, sparking renewed interest in unravelling the truth behind the incident. Some of these theories involved the possible involvement of the Central Intelligence Agency (CIA) in the tragic crash. A controversial revelation emerged in 2008 with the publication of alleged conversations between former CIA officer Robert T. Crowley, referred to as 'The Crow' within the agency, and journalist Gregory Douglas (born Peter Stahl). These discussions were chronicled in the book "Conversations with the Crow," stirring public suspicion and fostering belief in a potential CIA connection to the aircraft crash.

Crowley, known for his tenure in the Directorate of Plans, often colloquially labelled as the 'Department of Dirty Tricks,' spent his entire career with the CIA and had been a prominent figure since the agency's inception. Following Crowley's passing in October 2000, the book revealed that before his demise, he engaged in extensive conversations with Douglas and purportedly entrusted him with two lockers filled with documents, intended to be opened only after his death. The excerpted conversation in the book, supposedly occurring on July 5, 1996, highlighted Crowley's perspective on India's then Prime Minister Homi Bhabha's death and the circumstances surrounding it.

Within this conversation, Crowley alluded to past tensions between the United States and India during the 1960s. He referred to India's pursuit of developing an atomic bomb, expressing the struggles and disagreements between the two nations. Crowley recounted India's aspiration to assert its prowess as a global power, which had led to apprehensions and challenges for the United States. He hinted at India's associations with Russia, suggesting that the Indian pursuit of nuclear capabilities might have entangled the country in partnerships or alliances that troubled the American government.

The revelations attributed to Crowley's alleged conversation shed light on the intricate web of international relations and the Cold War era tensions, inferring the complex dynamics and geopolitical manoeuvres that might have influenced the aviation incidents and the broader political climate. The existence of such conversations has spurred ongoing debates and investigations, igniting curiosity about the intertwined narratives of aviation history and global politics during that period.

He labelled Bhabha as the 'chief expert' and declared that he had the ability to construct a bomb. According to him, Bhabha had been caution multiple times but ignored it due to his pride. He also made his ambition of obtaining nuclear parity with other powerful countries known. Furthermore, the speaker suggested that Bhabha could be dangerous. Unexpectedly, his Boeing 707 exploded in mid-flight to Vienna. Miraculously, there were no proof to the incident, which resulted in global safety.

Crowley boasted of the agency's power to blow up the plane over Vienna but preferred to cause a lesser tragedy of death among mountain goats. His knowledge on the KGB ran deep, and he had no qualms in connecting Shastri's assassination to them. Not only that, but he also accused the agency of causing Bhabha's untimely demise, calling him 'a genius who could get things done'. Comparing it to another tragic death, that of Enrico Mattei-an Italian oil magnate whose private plane was sabotaged by the CIA-, Crowley concluded that India had become much quieter after Bhabha. The dreadfulness of these acts weighed heavily on his words as he uttered them.

The truth behind these shocking claims remains uncertain, and it is likely that we will never know the real story. Douglas is a shady character at best – a Nazi-sympathiser, con artist, and Holocaust denier who has been implicated in forgery, as well as making other dubious revelations without any evidence.

Certainly, the Americans had no desire for India to acquire nuclear power, but even the most willing minds among us would find it hard to believe that such a massive amount of people (117 people) had to be sacrificed just to eliminate one individual.

The Bossons glacier in Chamonix, France, has been yielding unexpected artefacts related to India's historical nuclear endeavours, due to the effects of climate change causing the melting of the glacier. Among these discoveries are official documents marked 'top secret' and 'secret' originating from the Ministry of External Affairs, discovered alongside the wreckage of Air India flight 101. The remnants unearthed include an intriguing 19.8-pound bag labelled 'Diplomatic Mail Ministry of External Affairs', retrieved by a rescue worker in August 2012 and eventually returned to the Indian embassy in Paris. This container held an assortment of newspapers dating back to January 1966. Furthermore, the wreckage site at Mont Blanc has been a continued source of revelations, revealing an array of items such as letters, diplomatic papers, cameras, and jewellery.

These recovered documents, some of which are dated early 1966, encompass New Delhi's assessments of Chinese defence and nuclear capabilities. The material provides insight into Indian evaluations of Chinese foreign policy, particularly focused on Beijing's relationship with the West and the Sino-Soviet schism. Several documents originated from the Ministry of External Affairs' East Asia Division, exploring Indian analyses of Chinese defence production, missile development, and their nuclear weapons programme. There's a notable document from 20 January 1966, discussing the difficulty in producing an objective and accurate assessment of China's military capabilities due to the absence of official statistics. Another document mentioned Chinese advancements in nuclear delivery capability, indicating the potential reduction in bomb size by the end of 1966, making it deliverable by an IL-28 light bomber. The records suggest that China might possess a nuclear-armed missile with a range of 1,000 miles by mid-1967.

Moreover, these findings hint at lesser-known Indian deliberations on nuclear security guarantees during the Geneva-based discussions of the Eighteen Nations Disarmament Committee (ENDC), which eventually led to the creation of the Nuclear Non-proliferation Treaty. Of particular interest is the fact that the Air India flight crash occurred just days prior to the Ninth Session of the ENDC, raising the possibility that these discoveries could offer insights into the circumstances that may have influenced India's stand during these crucial discussions. Notably, VC Trivedi, India's ambassador to Switzerland and close associate of Dr. Homi Bhabha, played a significant role in these negotiations. About a month after the crash, Trivedi delivered a speech at the ENDC advocating for nuclear security guarantees for India from the superpowers, outside of alliance structures, as a prerequisite for signing the NPT. The documents discovered in Chamonix could provide clues and context about the discussions that led to such an action.

In the midst of an insightful review, Jayita Sarkar of Boston University encountered a cache of documents in mid-2017 during a meeting held in Geneva with Françoise Rey, a Chamonix-based novelist who has dedicated years to researching the mysteries surrounding the crash of flight 101. While Rey possesses a few official Indian documents, the majority are dispersed among residential homes in Chamonix and various other locations, discovered serendipitously by local residents hunting for 'treasures'. The crash sites themselves lie close to Nid d'Aigle, commonly known as the Eagle's Nest, the final stop on the tramway that ferries tourists to the base of Mont Blanc in France. It's also the point from which mountaineers commence their arduous ascent up the stunning heights of the Alps. The memorial inaugurated by Prime Minister Narendra Modi in August 2019 at Nid d'Aigle stands as a tribute to Bhabha and the victims of the two Air India crashes, marking their indelible place in history.

In a conversation with Indira Chowdhury, Jamshed Bhabha, in a poignant recollection, mentioned the critical role of fate in his uncle's untimely demise. He narrated how his mother grappled with the fact that Bhabha had been scheduled for a later flight but tragically decided to take the earlier one that met its tragic end. However, historical reports detail a different account. Bhabha had initially planned to fly on the plane departing from Bombay on January 22 but cancelled his trip at the last minute. The Statesman's report on the incident confirmed this, stating, 'Dr. Bhabha [...] had booked his passage on the plane which left Bombay on Saturday, January 22, but he cancelled at the eleventh hour to travel by the ill-fated Boeing.'

While Jamshed's recollections may have blurred over time, the actual records indicate that Bhabha was not originally intended to be on that doomed flight. This discrepancy leads to an unverified anecdote. RM Lala, a source, suggested a widely circulated belief that Pipsy Wadia might have been the reason behind Bhabha's late change of flight plans. While the precise cause of this change remains uncertain, it was believed that Meherbai, Bhabha's sister, held Pipsy accountable for this decision for the remainder of her life. The family received the distressing news through a phone call, where Jamshed initially struggled to accept the shocking reality, and his wife, Betty, eventually had to deliver the news to Meherbai.

Furthermore, journalist Shyam Bhatia speculated that Jamshed's personal animosity might have extended to Pipsy Wadia, shedding light on why he forcibly took away several of Bhabha's personal and professional papers from her home, even threatening to destroy them. Such complex familial dynamics, associated with the tragedy, have contributed to the unresolved questions and lingering speculations surrounding Bhabha's abrupt change in travel plans and the crash itself.

On the fateful day of Bhabha's demise, BV Sreekantan found himself at MIT, all set to partake in a colloquium centred on a topic that had deeply intrigued Bhabha — antimatter. The shocking news of Bhabha's passing reached Sreekantan through a phone call from Professor George Clark. Television and radio reports promptly confirmed the distressing event. Deeply affected, Sreekantan hurriedly sought out Professor Phil Morrison, the individual overseeing the colloquium, expressing his profound disturbance, saying, 'Sir, I am in such a state that I can't deliver this talk today; I am shaken to the core.' Professor Morrison, in response, encouraged Sreekantan, 'Don't forgo the talk. Dedicate it to his memory. I'm certain you will do fine.' Sreekantan, slightly encouraged, responded, 'Well, in that case, I will try.' He indeed delivered the presentation, which was well received. Subsequently, he hastened home, had a swift dinner, and retired to bed, deeply moved, shedding tears in the solitude of the night.

During that night, he had an unusual dream: Bhabha appeared, garbed in a traditional Parsi dagli (a white closed-collar coat) and cap, steering a golden chariot drawn by four white horses, soaring high above the sky. Sreekantan recounted that this dream provided an immediate solace, prompting him to awaken his wife and share the peculiar vision. He reckoned that this dream could have been a subconscious fusion influenced by his readings of the Bhagavad Gita: Bhabha assumed the role of his Krishna, and he saw himself as Bhabha's Arjuna.

The poignant memory also echoed for the computer scientist, S. Ramani, who reminisced about encountering NR Puthran, donning trousers instead of his usual holiday shorts, at the East Canteen. When questioned about the unexpected change in attire, Puthran sorrowfully relayed the grim news of the crash, evoking a profound personal loss. Ramani vividly recalled witnessing Bhabha in close proximity to Puthran just days before the tragic event. Bhabha had been visibly upset due to the issuance of orders to cut down some trees, marking an emotional imprint of the esteemed scientist's final days.

*****

Following Bhabha's untimely passing, the mantle of leading the AEC was initially extended to S Chandrasekhar by the Prime Minister's office. However, it came to light that Chandrasekhar was an American citizen, a fact that wasn't initially considered by the office. This unexpected revelation was shared during a special meeting between Chandrasekhar and Indira Gandhi following the second Nehru Memorial Lecture in November 1968. In this discourse, Chandrasekhar elucidated the circumstances surrounding his declination of the offered role, prompting Gandhi's response, 'Well, all this was not made clear to me.'

In the aftermath of Bhabha's passing, India found itself bereft of both its political and scientific leaders within a mere month. The succession of Vikram Sarabhai, a proponent of peace and an adherent of Gandhian ideals, to Bhabha's position was a rather peculiar choice. Sarabhai was an advocate for peace and was known to oppose the development of a nuclear weapons programme or the concept of a Peaceful Nuclear Explosion (PNE). His ascendancy to this role was met with doubts, considering his philosophy that developing nuclear armaments could significantly impede India's economic progress by diverting critical resources away from productive pursuits. Moreover, he didn't believe that simply detonating a bomb would serve as an effective nuclear deterrent. According to Sarabhai, achieving nuclear deterrence encompassed a complete defence mechanism, including means of delivery and long-range missiles, demanding substantial national resources.

Sarabhai, in his opposition to nuclear armament, cast doubts on the moral and practical utility of such weaponry. He took steps to redirect the focus away from the Peaceful Nuclear Explosive project conceptualised by Bhabha and the other scientists in the DAE. Though he didn't outrightly dismiss the idea of nuclear weapons for India, he was against the particular PNE envisioned by his predecessors, advocating for a more grounded, substantial approach rather than symbolic gestures.

Despite Sarabhai's attempts to shift the agenda, the PNE initiative persisted. The scientists in their research had a certain level of autonomy, enabling the continuation of bomb development. Even as Sarabhai attempted to transition the direction of the nuclear programme, he recognised the challenge of following in Bhabha's footsteps, expressing to the then-cabinet secretary, Dharam Vira, that it wasn't merely assuming a role but inheriting an entire ideology.

During his tenure as the head of the AEC, Vikram Sarabhai encountered challenges from Homi Sethna, who ardently believed he was the rightful heir to Bhabha's legacy and vigorously vied for the position. However, upon losing the contention, Sethna adopted a persistently confrontational stance against Sarabhai. He claimed that upon taking office, Sarabhai put an end to the Peaceful Nuclear Explosive Program (SNEPP) and demanded all related documents to be surrendered. Sarabhai, known for his avoidance of direct confrontation and preference for a more restrained approach, presumably attempted to build a rapport with Sethna. Nevertheless, Sethna, nursing a wounded ego from his unsuccessful bid, rebuffed Sarabhai, persistently opposing and provoking him at every available opportunity.

Raja Ramanna, during a private conversation, conceded that Sarabhai couldn't prevent the scientists from pursuing their work. This suggests that the scientists within the AEC might have continued their efforts on the bomb, whether clandestinely or openly. Sethna, heading the BARC at the time, sought explicit permission from Indira Gandhi to continue the work initially sanctioned during the Bhabha-Shastri compromise. PN Haksar, the Prime Minister's secretary, advised Gandhi on this matter, and she gave her decision. However, this decision did not directly translate into the conduct of a nuclear test since the official stance was that India would not fabricate a nuclear weapon.

The groundwork for the nuclear explosive tested at Pokhran commenced in 1968, under the supervision of Ramanna and R Chidambaram, alongside the collaboration of BD Nagchaudhuri, the director of DRDO. Approximately 50 to 75 scientists were actively involved in the nuclear explosives project. Although Sarabhai might have been aware of these activities, he seemingly chose not to intervene. According to a former atomic energy official cited by George Perkovich, Sarabhai refrained from halting the project, deeming it unsuitable for his style and inclinations as he wasn't willing to engage in that specific conflict.

The AEC was established with broader objectives than solely producing nuclear electricity. Its charter explicitly aimed at the development of atomic energy for multifaceted purposes. MR Srinivasan, who led the DAE in the 1980s, affirmed that the commission's stance on nuclear technology was centred on a country's independent pursuit for its own advantage, whether it was intended for peaceful or military applications. During this time, India took a more active role in the negotiations for a non-proliferation treaty.

VC Trivedi represented India in the Geneva discussions, advocating that if non-nuclear weapon states were expected to refrain from developing such armaments, the nuclear weapon states should freeze all activities linked to enhancing further nuclear weapons and their delivery systems. This appeal for universal nuclear disarmament unsettled both the United States and the Soviet Union. Negotiations surrounding the non-proliferation treaty occurred between 1965 and 1968, culminating in its signing on 1 July 1968. India chose not to become a signatory to this treaty.

Similar to Shastri, Sarabhai's opposition to the development of a 'peaceful' nuclear device weakened over time. During a speech at the Fourth International Conference on the Peaceful Uses of Atomic Energy in Geneva in September 1971, Sarabhai announced a shift in his scientists' focus, prioritising the development of Peaceful Nuclear Explosives (PNE). Tragically, a few months later, on 30 December 1971, Sarabhai passed away suddenly due to a heart attack at the age of 52. His successor, Homi Sethna, did not share the same reluctance towards nuclear explosions. During Sethna's tenure, India conducted its first nuclear test on 18 May 1974 in Pokhran, marking this event two and a half years after Sarabhai's untimely demise.

There's an intriguing anecdote in Ramanna's history involving an unexpected offer made by Saddam Hussein, the Iraqi dictator, after four years following the Pokhran blast. During his visit to Baghdad as Hussein's personal guest, Ramanna was given a tour of the city and Iraq's primary nuclear facility at Tuwaitha. After the tour, Hussein invited Ramanna to his office and asked him to take charge of Iraq's nuclear programme. Hussein offered, "I will pay you whatever you want." Feeling apprehensive, Ramanna swiftly left Iraq.

Homi J. Bhabha's office was located on the fourth floor of the Tata Institute of Fundamental Research (TIFR), with a view overlooking the sea. From this office, he oversaw the creation of the renowned Amoeba Garden on the institute's west lawn. It was a place where Bhabha conducted meetings with faculty and visitors, often causing a significant wait time for those seeking an audience with him. Following his passing, Bhabha's office was left unoccupied for over three decades.

MGK Menon, who shared late working hours with Bhabha in that office, was emotionally unprepared to take over his mentor's workspace. Similarly, Sreekantan, who succeeded Menon, declined to use the office despite JRD Tata's insistence. Instead, the room was utilised for council and other meetings. Even Jamshed Bhabha felt that the directors of TIFR should utilise what was once his brother's room, yet the leadership of TIFR decided to leave it vacant.

Successors like Virendra Singh also chose not to occupy Bhabha's office. It wasn't until 1997, when SS Jha became the director, that the space was finally utilised. Jha transformed Bhabha's office into a museum, relocating the furniture and other items to the museum area in the auditorium foyer. Objects like his desk, bookshelves, and the iconic Eero Saarinen Tulip chair, an emblem of mid-century modern furniture design, were displayed behind glass. This initiative was also supported by Jamshed Bhabha. However, during the celebration of Bhabha's centenary in 2009, the office's museum-like exhibition was dismantled, and the furniture was returned to its original place on the fourth floor of the institute.

❑